God's Plumb Line

Preaching From the Not-So-Minor Prophets

Alex A. Gondola Jr.

CSS Publishing Company, Inc.
Lima, Ohio

GOD'S PLUMB LINE

FIRST EDITION
Copyright © 2013
by CSS Publishing Co., Inc.

Published by CSS Publishing Company, Inc., Lima, Ohio 45807. All rights reserved. No part of this publication may be reproduced in any manner whatsoever without the prior permission of the publisher, except in the case of brief quotations embodied in critical articles and reviews. Inquiries should be addressed to: CSS Publishing Company, Inc., Permissions Department, 5450 N. Dixie Highway, Lima, Ohio 45807.

Unless otherwise marked, scripture quotations are from the New Revised Standard Version of the Bible. Copyright 1989 by the Division of Christian Education of the National Council of the Churches of Christ in the USA. Used by permission.

Scripture quotations marked The Message are taken from The Message by Eugene H. Peterson, copyright © 1993, 1994, 1995, 1996, 2000, 2001, 2002. Used by permission of NavPress Publishing Group. All rights reserved.

Scripture quotations marked RSV are from the Revised Standard Version of the Bible, Old Testament Section, Copyright 1952; New Testament Section, Second Edition© 1971 by the Division of Christian Education of the National Council of the Churches of Christ in the USA. Used by permission.

Scripture quotations marked KJV are from the King James Version of the Bible, in the public domain.

Scripture quotations marked NIV are taken from Holy Bible, New International Version, copyright © 1973, 1978, 1984 International Bible Society. Used by permission of Zondervan Bible Publishers. All rights reserved.

Library of Congress Cataloging-in-Publication Data

Gondola, Alex A.
  God's plumb line : preaching from the not-so-minor Prophets / Alex Gondola. -- FIRST EDITION.
    pages cm
  Includes bibliographical references.
  ISBN 0-7880-2722-0 (alk. paper)
  1. Bible. Minor prophets--Criticism, interpretations, etc. I. Title.

BS1560.G66 2013
224'.906--dc23   2013005091

For more information visit www.csspub.com or call (800) 241-4056.

ISBN-13: 978-0-7880-2722-2
ISBN-10: 0-7880-2722-0   PRINTED IN USA

Dedicated to

Gabriel Fackre

*a prophetic witness and inspiration
to decades of
Andover Newton Theological School Students,
the United Church of Christ
and the Church worldwide*

Acknowledgments

This author claims no special expertise in the Hebrew Scriptures: just introductory, survey classes taken as an undergraduate and in seminary, plus almost four decades of preaching experience, and a desire to learn. The foundation for this book was an independent study in the Hebrew Scriptures I completed through the Design for Leadership program of Defiance College in Defiance, Ohio. I recommend this well-established distance learning program as a good resource for continuing education for pastors. Julie Fritz-Bergman, an Adjunct Professor who teaches Old Testament classes at Defiance College, reviewed the manuscript. Some of her comments have been incorporated.

Sample discussion questions follow each sermon. The questions were designed by Dr. Marilyn Fenton, Associate Professor of Education at Southern New Hampshire University. I am grateful to Professor Fritz-Bergman and Dr. Fenton for their contributions. Any shortcomings in this volume are mine. Several improvements are theirs.

God's Plumb Line: Preaching from the Not-So-Minor Prophets became the basis for a sermon series I preached once a month over a calendar year at Saint Paul United Church of Christ in Wapakoneta, Ohio. I am grateful to my former congregation for welcoming this and the many other sermon series I preached there during my years as their Senior Pastor. I also am grateful for the encouragement I have received from the members and friends of First Congregational Church

(United Church of Christ) of Milford, New Hampshire. This helped me to complete this book while serving in a new position for me — my first-ever interim pastorate.

It has been a privilege to work again with CSS Publishing Company. I am grateful for the efforts CSS President David Runk and Editor Missy Cotrell have made to bring this book to publication. CSS remains what it has been for more than four decades: a reliable resource and a source of inspiration for pastors, Christian educators, and congregations across America and worldwide.

Table of Contents

Preface — 9

Overview of Amos — 11
God's Plumb Line
(Amos 7:7-14)

Overview of Hosea — 23
Love Story
(Hosea 11:1-4, 7-9)

Overview of Jonah — 35
Jonah Is No Fish Story!
(Jonah 3:1-10)

Overview of Micah — 47
What Does the Lord Require?
(Micah 6:1-8)

Overview of Zephaniah — 57
What Goes Around, Comes Around: God Is Not Mocked
(Zephaniah 3:14-18a)

Overview of Nahum — 69
Lest We Forget
(Nahum 1:2-7)

Overview of Obadiah — 83
When Families Fight
(Obadiah 10-15)

Overview of Habakkuk   95
How to Get Your Prayers Answered
(Habakkuk 3:2, 17-19)

Overview of Malachi   107
Don't Rob God!
(Malachi 3:8-12)

Overview of Haggai   119
These ARE the Good Old Days!
(Haggai 2:1-5)

Overview of Zechariah   133
Behold, Your King Is Coming!
(Zechariah 9:9-10)

Overview of Joel   145
Good News, Bad News, Who's to Say?
(Joel 2:1-3, 10-14a)

Annotated Bibliography   157

Preface

Many of us learned the books of the Bible as children. The twelve Minor Prophets always fascinated me. Who *were* these characters with the difficult-to-pronounce, exotic-sounding names? We learned about Daniel and Jonah in Sunday school. But who were Obadiah, Habakkuk, Zephaniah, and Haggai? Many children do not know these prophets' circumstances, messages, or life stories. Nor may many adults.

One problem is the Minor Prophets don't come up very often in the Revised Common Lectionary. Amos appears in the three-year cycle seven times. That's the most. Habakkuk, Haggai, and Zechariah are the first reading only once every three years. Obadiah and Nahum aren't chosen at all. Therefore, lectionary preachers are not directed to these books.

A related issue is a relative lack of resources. There are numerous good books, journals, and websites that follow the lectionary. So much so that sometimes the lectionary preacher suffers from what Voltaire called an "embarrassment of riches." There can be so much to preach on and so many worthwhile themes, it's hard to choose.

Because the Minor Prophets are so infrequently the assigned reading, these "lection-aides" are not available. In an attempt to address this imbalance in resources, an Annotated Bibliography has been added. Hymn suggestions, discussion questions, and idea starters for children's lessons also are provided for each sermon. These may assist the busy pastor in his or her worship or Bible Study planning.

This slim volume is offered as an aide to sermon preparation and/or a source for devotional reading and/or a resource for Bible Study. Hopefully the reader will discover the Minor Prophets are not so minor. This should be no surprise. First, because "all scripture is inspired by God and is useful for teaching, for reproof, for correction, and for training in righteousness..." (2 Timothy 3:16). Second, because we too need the prophetic word to guide us as we face the challenges and opportunities of our time.

— Overview —
AMOS

The prologue (1:1) states Amos prophesied during the kingships of Jeroboam II in Israel and Uzziah in Judah. The dates of his call and ministry are difficult to fix exactly. Some scholars place Amos' prophetic ministry as early as 760 BCE, others around 740 or the late 730s. In any case it's clear the northern kingdom was enjoying a period of great prosperity, peace, and ease. But this also was a time of great social and economic inequality and moral laxity.

The prophet himself was a native of Tekoa, a village southeast of Bethlehem in Judah, the southern kingdom. Amos states he was not born into the prophetic "guild," nor did he train for it. Rather Amos was a layman, a (seemingly) simple herdsman and dresser of sycamore trees whom God called and commissioned to preach to Israel in the north (6:14-15). As with other prophets, Amos' calling came with a feeling of compulsion: "The Lord God has spoken; who can but prophesy?" he asks in 38b. Also, like other prophets, Amos receives visions, five in all: of swarming locusts, a shower of fire, a plumb line held against a wall (7:1-9), a basket of summer fruit (8:1-3), and the utter destruction of Israel (9:1-4). Many of Amos' words such as his exchange with Amaziah, the priest, indicate a straightforward, fiery personality (7:10-17). Yet the prophet does not lack compassion, for he beseeches God to spare Israel and God relents (7:4b).

Hymns related to Amos include John Rippon's venerable "How Firm a Foundation," "Ye Saints of the Lord," which could be connected to the prophet's vision of a plumb line in 7:7-9, and Jane Huber Parker's contemporary hymn "Let Justice Flow Like Streams" based, in part, on verse 24, "(L)et justice roll down like waters, and righteousness like an ever-flowing stream." This may be sung to the familiar tune "Saint Thomas S.M." Amos himself appears to quote stanzas of a hymn or hymns from his era. Commentators have reconstructed a hymn from verses 4:13; 5:5-6; 9:5-6.

A plumb bob could be used as an illustration for a children's lesson. Many antique stores will have one to borrow or buy. The pulpit might be measured against it, to see if it's "on the level." Or modern leveling tools, like laser or spirit levels, could be introduced, explained, and tested with comments on the importance of level foundations and walls. Afterward the children might be reminded we too need to build our lives on the firm foundation of God's word.

God's Plumb Line
Amos 7:7-14

Amos wasn't born a prophet, but he *was* a farmer. And many farmers are pretty handy at building things, aren't they? A farmer is a "Jack of all trades," and master of many. We have farmers in our congregation. I checked with some. They've poured foundations, designed and built sheds, put additions on their houses, assembled windmills, built garages, and raised barns. The quintessential farmers/builders are the Amish. They're noted for the quality of their construction: remarkable, since it's often done without power tools!

Like most farmers, Amos knew something about building. He understood the importance of keeping foundations level and walls plumb. Today we use spirit levels and laser levels to keep things vertically and horizontally straight. These are examples of each.

In Amos' day a plumb bob was one of the few leveling tools available. Here's one *(show tool)*. A plumb bob goes back to the ancient Egyptians. It is hung from a high spot on your structure. Gravity pulls the weight straight down. As you build, moving up, you measure your structure against the line to see if it's vertical.

If a building isn't plumb, straight up and down, its walls will be weak and begin to buckle, because they can't support the weight. The wall will fall and the building will collapse.

Perhaps Amos, our farmer/builder, was working on a wall when he received his vision. He was struggling to line up a wall. Suddenly Amos realized if a builder has high standards, certainly God's standards must be higher. God was measuring Israel against a plumb line, just like Amos was using a plumb line. "See, I am setting a plumb line in the midst of my people, Israel," says God, speaking through the prophet (Amos 7:8b). God's people were being measured — and they were found to be crooked.

Where was ancient Israel "out of line"? For one thing, lots of Israelites were addicted to luxury and sunk in self-indulgence. Trusting in their wealth, they forgot their need for God.

Amos attacked their attitudes like this: "Woe to those who lie on beds of ivory, and lounge on their couches, and eat lambs from the flock and calves from the stall; who sing idle songs to the sound of the harp... who drink wine from bowls, and anoint themselves with the finest oils" (vv. 4-6a). God was angry because Israel was going soft.

In another place the prophet compares the women of Samaria to fat cows grazing. "Listen to this, you cows of Basham," he shouts, "indolent and pampered..." (4:1 The Message). Amos, a southerner, called northern women "cows"! That didn't make him friends. It would be like someone from the Deep South going to New England and saying its lovely ladies look like livestock.

Along with Israel's greed and laziness went sexual sins, and elders misleading and perverting youngsters (2:7b and 12a, respectively). Just as bad as these "sins of the flesh" were corruption and bribery in the courts (5:12b) and economic injustice.

"They'd sell a poor man for a pair of shoes... They drive the penniless into the dirt, shove the luckless into a ditch. They'd sell their own grandmother," complained Amos (2:6b-7). He continued, "(Y)ou run roughshod over the poor and take the bread right out of their mouths" (5:11 The Message).

The God of the Bible is vitally concerned with how the least and last are treated in any society. The measure of a nation is not how powerful or how wealthy it is. It's whether or not it takes care of its outcasts and the poor. In Isaiah God says, "I'll make justice the measuring stick and righteousness the plumb line..." (28:17 The Message). God's people were lined up against God's plumb line of righteousness and justice and found lacking. They had to straighten up.

Because Israel wasn't just, God wasn't pleased with their worship. Their gatherings in the temples, and their offerings, without righteousness, made God sick. Some of Amos' strongest attacks arrive in chapter 5. God is speaking, through the prophet.

God says,

> *I hate, I despise your feasts, and I take no delight in your solemn assemblies. Even though you offer me your burnt offerings and grain offerings, I will not accept them; and the offerings of well-being of your fatted animals I will not look upon. Take away from me the noise*

> *of your songs; I will not listen to the melody of your harps. But let justice roll down like waters, and righteousness like an everflowing stream.*
> (5:21-24)

So it wasn't just the commoners who were corrupt. The religious establishment was rotten too, like Amaziah, the priest, who confronted Amos and told him to go home. Honest, straight-talking priests and prophets were so rare in Israel that God had to import them from the south. That's a warning to preachers like me. If we don't preach God's word, we will be judged.

Amos dared speak the truth to power, even ugly truths about Israel's failed religion. He knew full well he would be attacked. For, as Amos puts it, "Raw truth is never popular" (5:10 The Message). Like many farmers, Amos wasn't shy about speaking his mind. He was down to earth and told it like he saw it with earthy speech.

What would please God, if God wasn't happy with empty worship? Nothing less than this. Amos said, "Let justice roll down like waters, and righteousness like an everflowing stream." That's maybe the most important line in Amos, "Let justice roll down like waters, and righteousness like an everflowing stream" (5:21-24 RSV). You might remember Martin Luther King Jr. quoted that line in his last speech, the night before he was killed. In another place Amos demanded, "Seek good, and not evil, and you may live..." (5:14 RSV).

The situation was critical. Israel was like a dangerous, tottering wall. God, the builder, had measured them against a plumb line and found them lacking. Sometimes the best thing you can do with a bad wall is tear it down and start over again. Ask a farmer.

That's what Amos the farmer/prophet was warning Israel would happen. God was about to dismantle their nation. There would be no escape. It would be as if a man ran away from a lion at night, and instead ran into a hungry bear, said Amos. Or made it to his house safely, only to put his hand on a poisonous snake in the dark (5:19).

Truth be told, the book of Amos is mostly gloom and doom. Its 141 verses focused on Israel's failures and judgment, and only five hopeful ones at the end.

That was Amos' message 760 years before Christ. What does this straight-talking farmer have to say to us today? The same things! God's word doesn't change. But now God's plumb line is applied to us. How well do you and I, and our nation, measure up? Remember, a plumb line doesn't lie!

Would God measure our love of comfort and ease and find us wanting? Are we so addicted to material things that we forget about God? Of course, our economy is down right now. Unlike the ancient Israelites in Amos' day, many aren't lying in the lap of luxury, on "ivory couches."

But are we still possessed by our possessions — overly worried about what we don't have and not trusting God will provide? Jesus said, "(D)o not worry about your life, what you will eat or what you will drink, or about your body, what you will wear. Is not life more than food, and the body more than clothing?" He continued, famously,

"Look at the birds of the air; they neither sow nor reap nor gather into barns (an image any farmer could understand), and yet your heavenly Father feeds them. Are you not of more value than they?" (Matthew 6:25-26).

Trusting God and God's goodness should be a firm foundation for all of us in prosperity and in adversity. The economy might have changed, but God hasn't. Are we living up to the motto on our coins, "In God We Trust"?

God also holds a plumb line against our families. God sees their brokenness, their tensions, the way we sometimes fight. The Ten Commandments tell us "honor your father and mother." Ephesians advises wives to support and understand their husbands, and husbands to "go all out" for their wives. Parents are not to "exasperate" their children or "provoke" them "to anger" (Ephesians 5:22, 25; 6:1 The Message; also 6:1 NRSV).

Every Christian family is supposed to be a miniature church, a Body of Christ, where each member is loved and valued. The late John Paul II called our homes "the domestic church."

But are our families filled with Christian love? If God measured our home life against the plumb line of God's word, would God find us wanting — wanting more of the acceptance, tolerance, and patience we are supposed to give?

God also holds a plumb line against our business dealings. Amos was shocked by the use of false measures, dishonest selling, and abuses of the poor. If God were to put a level against our nation and our finances, would we come out crooked?

Shortchanging customers, producing inferior products, stealing from the boss, goofing off on the job, and cheating on our taxes are all theft. Are our business practices in line? We don't have to be as big a crook as the convicted financier Bernie Madoff to be crooked.

Are we seeking justice for the least and the last in America? Amos might well be shocked by the way our (mostly) wealthy society still has an underclass. In fact, the number of American children going to bed hungry at night has grown in the last year. That, by the way, is also true in our city, where families served by our local food banks are up by 50%.

This ad once ran in a local paper. It was about hunger in America, and read "HUNGER: It's a problem when you are a child who can't concentrate in school because he didn't eat dinner last night (or when) you are elderly and must choose between food and life-sustaining medicine (or when) you are a single parent who wonders whether to pay her electricity bill or buy food." Those are real problems for real people, right here, right now.

What would God say about our worship? Would God be pleased with our Sunday songs and offerings? Or are we going through the motions without real conviction? Does what we hear on Sunday "spill over" into Monday? Do we drink so deeply at the well of worship that justice rolls down like water and righteousness like an ever-flowing stream the rest of the week? Would someone know you've been to church by the way you treat the needy? How does our worship measure up?

Another question sums them all up. If you or

I were put on trial for being a Christian, would there be enough evidence to convict us? Tough questions prompted by Amos, that plain-talking farmer. There's no place in our lives where God's plumb line doesn't apply and nowhere to hide.

Truth be told, most of us, much of the time, come out a little bit crooked; sometimes more than a bit. If we're honest, we have to admit that we don't always measure up. When we're out-of-line, something in our lives is sure to crumble. No happy life can be built with weak walls or a bad foundation.

But in the end Amos was hopeful. After nine chapters of anger and judgment, the prophet saw some light. There's a day coming when God will "restore" the "house that has fallen," when God will "repair the holes in the roof, replace the broken windows (and) fix it up like new" (Amos 9:11 The Message). That comes from chapter 9, the end of the book of Amos.

The New Revised Standard Version of the Bible titles this section, "The Restoration of David's Kingdom." The restoration of David's kingdom. For Christians, the restoration of David's kingdom is the coming of Christ. Jesus is David's descendant. He's the new yardstick you and I measure ourselves against. His words and example are the plumb line we must meet.

Clearly, we all come up short when measured against Jesus' perfection. Yet the same carpenter who points out our crookedness is also our Savior; a firm foundation, a cornerstone (1 Peter 2:6), upon which we can build.

Standing alone, none of us will ever measure up. But built on a foundation of faith in Jesus

Christ, with the help of the Holy Spirit, we can be straightened morally, day by day. Theologians call this "sanctification."

> *How firm a foundation, you saints of the Lord, Is laid for your faith in (God's) excellent word (Jesus being the Word)! What more can God say than to you (God) has said, To you, who for refuge to Jesus have fled?*
> (John Rippon, 1787)

Everything depends on what — or who — we choose to build on. Laziness, lies, and lovelessness will not long stand, but faith in Christ is a firm foundation. Amos, the farmer/builder/prophet, just might say "Amen!" to that.

Questions for Discussion

1. How does the metaphor/imagery of a plumb line resonate with us as Christians? What does "being out of plumb" mean to you as an individual? As a congregation? As a society?

2. How do we determine "plumb" to God?

3. Which aspects of our society have "gone soft," in your estimation?

4. Whose voices can proclaim and reproach in our society? What can we do to re-establish God's purpose in our times?

5. Explain how Jesus addresses the concerns voiced in Amos. How does Jesus provide a "new yardstick"?

6. Although we cannot match Jesus' plumb line, how can we still use him as a cornerstone? What role will Jesus' life and the Holy Spirit play in your life?

7. What does Amos gain in his instruction by being a simple man and a prophet?

— Overview —
HOSEA

Hosea comes before Amos in the Christian scriptures, but his call and ministry were chronologically later and longer than Amos'. Both prophesied to Israel, the northern kingdom, during the reigns of Jeroboam II in the north and Uzziah in Judah, the south. However, verse 1:1 of his book tells us Hosea continued preaching during the kingships of Jotham, Ahaz, and Hezekiah in Judah. This indicates an active ministry of several decades, beginning perhaps as early as 750 BCE — but ending before the fall of Israel to Assyria in 721 BCE, an event Hosea does not mention. Unlike Amos, Hosea was a northern native prophesying to his own people. In contrast with Amos, Hosea preached not only in times of prosperity but also during the social and political disruptions that followed Jeroboam II's death and the subsequent assassinations of four Israelite kings in fourteen years.

Little is known about Hosea's background except he was the son of Beeri (1:1). Some scholars find indications Hosea knew the priesthood from the inside out in verses 4:6-14, 5:1, 6:9, and 8:1. They speculate Hosea may have been a priest. But this is unproven. While Hosea's early years are unclear, his later family life is well known. The prophet, plus his errant wife Gomer, and their three famously — or infamously — named children, Jezreel ("God Sows" or maybe "Cast Away"), Lo-ruhamah ("Not Pitied"), and Lo-ammi ("Not My People") make up one of the Bible's most distinctive family groupings. Hosea uses their domestic drama as signs of God's judgment on and love for his wayward, adulterous people. James Montgomery Boice labeled Hosea, "the second greatest story in the Bible," eclipsed only by the incarnation, life, death, and resurrection of Jesus himself. Such is the power of this small book.

Some of the most beloved hymns in Christian hymnody can be related to Hosea. They include Fanny Crosby's "I Am Yours, O Lord"; Charlotte Elliott's "Just as I Am"; George Matheson's "O Love that Wilt not Let Me Go"; and Charles Wesley's "Love Divine, All Loves Excelling." Plus the life stories of Crosby, Elliott, Matheson, and Wesley are nearly as dramatic as Hosea's.

If one Minor Prophet is preached on every month, according to this order, Hosea falls in February. Valentine's Day could provide a lead in for the children's lesson. Get a package of little candy hearts with sayings and pass them out to the children. Note the sentiments like "Sweet Talk," "Be My Valentine," "Heat Wave," "You're Mine," and "Luv U." An attraction between two people can seem sweet. Unfortunately, it also can melt away like Valentine's Day candy. Contrast this with God's love for us, which is never ending and continues in good times and bad.

Love Story
Hosea 11:1-4, 7-9

What do you consider the greatest love story ever? I suppose what we consider a great love story depends on our taste. For some, the greatest love stories are on film, classics like *Casablanca* with Bergman and Bogie, or *The Quiet Man* with John Wayne and Maureen O'Hara. Maybe you prefer a more modern tearjerker like *Love Story* with Ryan O'Neil and Ali McGraw. Remember the line, "Love means never having to say you're sorry"? Or *Titanic* with Leonardo DiCaprio and Kate Winslet. Recall the young lovers' sinking feelings?

For others, the greatest love stories are found in Shakespeare: his plays, like *Romeo and Juliet* or some of his sonnets. For some "true love" is best portrayed in Gothic romances, like *Jane Eyre*. For others, the best love stories come from real life, like Edward VIII giving up a kingdom for Wallis Simpson, "the woman he loved." This love story came home to me once while on vacation in Florida. We had lunch at the old inn where Wallis and Edward were married and saw their honeymoon suite. Some prefer the love stories of Harlequin romances.

What do you consider the greatest love story ever? I think the greatest love stories are in the Bible. We don't always associate God's love with the prophets. Still, love stories are found in Hosea, the not-so-minor prophet we look at today.

In his book, the prophet provides three examples of God's love for Israel. By extension, these are examples of God's love for you and me. Two are quite common. They're drawn from everyday life. We read these illustrations and get it. One is shocking. Let's consider these three love stories in turn.

In Hosea chapter 11 (vv. 1-4, 7-9), Hosea says God loves Israel, and you and me, the way a parent loves a child. God's parental love is a familiar theme. Listen to these touching verses, from a modern paraphrase, The Message. God is speaking: "When Israel was only a child, I loved him," God says. "I called out, 'My son!' — called him out of Egypt (that's the Exodus). But when others called him, he ran off and left me." (Picture an ornery two-year-old, stubbornly running away from his parents on stubby, chubby legs.)

God continues, speaking through Hosea, "(H)e played at religion with toy gods. Still, I stuck with him (like any loving parent would). I rescued him from... bondage, but he never acknowledged my help." (Have your children ever been ungrateful to you, after all you have done?)

God continues, "He never admitted I was the one who was pulling his wagon (a great childhood image), that I lifted him up, like a baby to my cheek (as a mother cuddles her child), that I bent down to feed him (another mothering image)... My people are hell-bent on leaving me. They pray to (other gods) for help (clearly God is hurt by their betrayal)... But how can I give up on (my child)? How can I turn you loose, Israel? I can't bear (even to) think such thoughts. My insides churn in protest. (S)o I'm not going to act on my anger. I'm not going to destroy (Israel). And why? Because I am God and not a human," Hosea concludes. "I'm the Holy One and I'm here — in your very midst."

That's a passage overflowing with parental love; plus a parent's disappointment and pain. Parents want the best for their children, don't they? But sometimes their children turn away. There's a Hebrew word *shub*, which means to "turn around." We *shub* God.

God bids us to come to him so he can give us something good. God wants to lift us close and cuddle us and feed us on his word. But, like willful toddlers, we sometimes turn around and run in the other direction. We even head, like a two-year-old can, for danger.

A two-year-old may not know better. But you and I do! This passage speaks of God's patient, long-suffering love. A love that will not let us go even when we turn our backs on God. It hurts God when we reject him, like a parent is hurt. But God's love is such that God does not give up on us. That's the first love story in Hosea. God loves us with the patient, long-suffering love any good parent gives their child — a love that searches after them even when they go astray.

Beyond this, Hosea says God's love for us is like the love of a husband courting his wife. Several verses in Hosea, chapter 2, portray God like this. God is speaking, again in The Message: "(H)ere's what I'm going to do: I'm going to start all over again. I'm taking (Israel) back into the wilderness where we had our first date, and I'll court her."

(That's a reference to the forty years God and Israel spent in the desert: a long courtship!) "I'll give her bouquets of roses. I'll turn Heartbreak Valley into Acres of Hope. She'll respond like she did as a young girl, those days when she was fresh out of Egypt. At that time... (she'll) address (God as), 'My Dear husband!'" (2:14-15).

Then, later in the same passage, God is speaking: "I'll marry you for good — forever"! I'll marry you true and proper, in love and tenderness. Yes, I'll marry you and neither leave you nor let you go. You'll know me, God, for who I really am" (2:19-20 The Message).

God as husband is less familiar than God as parent. But this, also, is in the Bible. The Old Testament, the Hebrew Scriptures, speaks of God as a loving spouse to Israel. Consider Isaiah 62:5b: "(A)s a bridegroom is happy in his bride, so your God is happy with you" (The Message). Since the Middle Ages, the Song of Songs has been read as an analogy of Christ, the Bridegroom's, love for his church. Jesus even calls himself the Bridegroom in Matthew (9:14-15; 25:1-13).

Ephesians says the church is married to Christ (5:25, 27, 29-32). Revelation chapter 19 portrays joy at a wedding feast, when Christ, the Bridegroom and his bride, the Church, are united in heaven. Like a bride, believers in heaven will wear radiant white (19:7-8). There's a different love story here. It's more the love of equals, the love of a husband for a wife. Still, we understand the point.

But now we come to something in Hosea that's shocking and has breathtaking implications. God's love for you and me is like that of a husband or wife whose partner has committed adultery and who takes the adulterer back! Could anything be more painful than having a cheating spouse? Unfortunately, the prophet Hosea did.

I've got to tell you, Hosea's marriage looked pretty rocky from the start. God commanded him to take Gomer, a prostitute, for a wife. Anyone my age can't hear that name and not think of Gomer Pyle from *The Andy Griffith Show*. But Gomer was a *woman*'s name in Hosea's day — and Gomer of Mayberry and Gomer, wife of Hosea, probably couldn't be more different. This "fallen woman" became the mother of Hosea's three children (1:2).

Hosea loved Gomer deeply. Maybe he thought tenderness and devotion would change her wayward heart. But Gomer continued to chase other men. There even were questions about whether or not Hosea's children were actually his. Ouch! That's painful!

It appears at some point Gomer left Hosea, probably for a lover. She got in debt and sold herself into slavery. That was a common way of paying off debt in ancient times. And you thought having a high credit card balance was bad!

Hosea could have said, "Good riddance to bad rubbish!" and written off Gomer. No one would have blamed him. Still God commanded Hosea to buy his wife back. Chapter 3 of Hosea shows the prophet in the humiliating position of bidding for his own wife at a slave auction. You can imagine the wagging tongues! Hosea looked like a fool in public, spending good money on her!

In those days, slaves were sold naked, so buyers could see exactly what they were getting. (This also was the case in the antebellum South, indicating not much progress in human rights in 2,600 years!) Gomer was on the auction block, stark naked. It was an age when people covered up more than today. Everyone saw her shame. She was a handsome woman. Men made comments and ogled. The bidding started. Imagine the scene.

"Who will give five silver shekels for this fine lady?" (I wondered how much five silver shekels were worth. So I looked it up in a Bible dictionary. It told me, helpfully, it's the equivalent of 100 gerahs. So, I still don't know. But it sounds like a lot!)

A leering guy next to Hosea shoots his hand up. Hosea counter-bids, "Seven shekels." His competitor bumps it to nine. Hosea counters with ten. The other guy goes to twelve.

Hosea ends the bidding with a shout, "Fifteen shekels of silver, eight bushels of barley, and all the wine from my vineyard" (3:2). Hosea was willing to pay big bucks to buy back his wandering wife! He pays the fee, covers her nakedness with his robe, and tenderly takes a weeping Gomer home. That's a real love story, friends!

The point here is not the state of Hosea's marriage but our relationship to God. God loves you and me with a long-suffering love, like Hosea loved Gomer. God sticks with us through thick and thin, like the prophet stuck with his wife. God loves us "for better or worse," and goes to great lengths to "buy us back" from slavery to sin, when our disobedience lands us in trouble — as it always does.

You and I have abandoned God, chasing after false gods. What are some of the false gods we run after in the post-modern world? Some folks park their god in their garage. They're consumed with their car: washing it, waxing it, vacuuming it, smoothing out the scratches. For some men, sometimes "god" is spelled "truck." Others float their god out on the ocean or one of the Great Lakes. Someone, probably a boat owner, once said, "You don't own a boat. With all the maintenance and expense, the boat owns you!" Someone else said a boat is a hole in the water into which you pour money.

Some make a god out of their home. They use only the back door and eat only in the kitchen so they won't mess up the dining room furniture or drag dirt across the carpet. Some of us have made a god out of our career. We pursue success at any cost. Sometimes, especially in tough times, financial security becomes our small-g god. We obsess over money.

A person or a relationship can occupy a god-like place in our lives. We worship the ground on which our beloved walks. We may have him or her constantly on our mind. I once counseled a young man who was so smitten with a young woman that even when he was away from her, the power of her presence, his strong feelings for her, filled the entire sky. Or, so he said.

We can make a false god out of our health, becoming obsessed with exercise, diet, vitamins, fitness. We can make a false god out of golf, a hobby, or a favorite player or team. We can become addicted to, or make a false god out of, alcohol, sex, pornography, or drugs.

We can make a false god out of a grudge, holding it until it begins to consume us. There's the story about an old man who held a grudge against his neighbor for decades. Sick and expecting to die, he called his estranged neighbor to his bedside. "I want you to know, I forgive you for what you did to me," he said. "But, if I get better," he continued, "I'm taking it all back."

Do members of the clergy chase after false gods? You bet! Gather any group of pastors together and before too long you are likely to see evidence of the little clergy gods. Who has a bigger church or better church attendance, a bigger mission budget or a larger church staff? Who published recently in some influential journal? Who attended the most prestigious schools? These are the false gods of clergy "success."

Anything or anyone that dominates our lives or captures our attention more than God is a false god. You've got yours. I've got mine. We run after them and that offends and wounds the living God, like Gomer's adultery hurt Hosea. Yet... the good news is that Hosea bought her back. God stops at nothing to buy us back.

We know what Hosea paid for Gomer. How far will God go to redeem you and me? Jesus paid the ultimate price for us in his blood on the cross. He bought us back from slavery to sin on the cross. Then he wrapped our nakedness with the robes of his righteousness. There is no greater love than this.

"For God so loved the world that he gave his only Son, that whoever believes in him should not perish but have eternal life" (John 3:16 RSV). There are love stories and then there is The Love

Story. Hosea hints at, and the gospel proclaims, the greatest love story ever told. God loves you and me like a parent loves a child, like a husband woos a wife. God even takes us back when we betray God by being unfaithful. Not every human spouse would do that or necessarily should. But God does. God pays the ultimate price to redeem us. That's "Love Divine."

Questions for Discussion

1. Compare and contrast the three concepts of love. What does each one say about human beings? How does God's response affect our response to him?

2. What are some of the false gods we run after in the post-modern world?

3. How do we explain the differences in the character of God told through different prophets? Read Jeremiah, for example. How can a God of vengeance be the same as Hosea's God of love?

— Overview —
JONAH

Jonah is unique among the Minor Prophets. The other eleven books are principally collections of oracles. They present the word of God as delivered through the prophet, but provide little background about the speaker's motivations, actions, or setting. In contrast, Jonah's preaching is indicated by just eight words, "Yet forty days, and Nineveh shall be overthrown!" (3:4). Instead this book is a story about a prophet. As such, Jonah has more in common with the narratives about Elijah and Elisha in 1 and 2 Kings than with the other Minor Prophets. His character and story are well developed and rightly are considered world literature.

As with Amos and Hosea, it's difficult to date the writing of Jonah exactly. Three verses place this story in the early decades of the eighth century. Jonah 1:1 tells us the prophet was "the son of Amittai." Second Kings 14:25 elaborates. It also names Amittai as Jonah's father, and adds Jonah was born in Gath-hepher, about three miles from Nazareth in the northern kingdom. It additionally states Jonah prophesied against the evils of Jeroboam II, who ruled in the north from 786 to 746 BCE. Jonah 1:2 calls Nineveh "a great city." But Nineveh was not ascendant until after 745

BCE and did not become Assyria's capitol until the reign of Sennacherib in 705-681 BCE. Taken together, 2 Kings 14:25 and Jonah 1:1-2 indicate Jonah's prophetic ministry in Israel took place sometime toward the end of Jeroboam II's reign, perhaps 750 BCE. His mission to Nineveh must have come years later.

Unfortunately, this time line doesn't fit Jonah's theology, which better reflects the post-exilic period. He presents a universalistic understanding of God. On the one hand, God's mercy is extended to all. God offers the opportunity to repent and be saved even to wicked Nineveh, the cruel oppressor of God's people — and Nineveh responds! This, plus the piety of the pagan sailors who were more pious than the prophet himself, crying out to God in prayer and throwing Jonah overboard only as a last resort, indicate a wider understanding of God. God is more than just the national God of Israel. For the author of Jonah, God is sovereign over all of nature and every nation. This theological perspective developed only after the exile, perhaps between 500 and 450 BCE. Clearly the book of Jonah was written much later than 750 BCE but was set in that earlier time for effect. Perhaps like the author of Ruth, which may have come from the same era, this unnamed writer wanted to make a point. God's power and love are universal. No one and no nation lie beyond God's concern.

Hymn suggestions for Jonah sermons include Isaac Watt's "I Sing the Mighty Power of God," plus two contemporary hymns: Jane Parker Huber's "Called as Partners in Christ's Service" and

Fred Kaan's "Help Us Accept Each Other."

A children's lesson might revolve around teaching the children the song "Jonah and the Whale." It's sung to the tune, "I'm a Little Teapot," and can be found online. Or connections could be made to Nancy E. Kurlik's well-known book *Free Willie*, which became the basis for the popular Warner Brothers film of the same name. Dankin makes a "Free Willie" plush toy that should be readily available. The point might be the story of a "whale" swallowing a man is unbelievable. Even more astonishing is God's love for us.

Jonah Is No Fish Story!
Jonah 3:1-10

Certain Bible names just seem to go together, don't they? When I say Adam, what do you think of? Eve. Cain and Abel, Noah and the Ark, Samson and Delilah, David and Goliath, Daniel and the Lion's Den. Jehoiachin and Zerubbabel. (Okay, so maybe you didn't get that last one. I had to look it up myself.)

But what do you think of when I say Jonah? Usually it's the whale. A man being swallowed whole by a whale and coming out alive! Pretty exciting stuff! Long before the Bible was written, the Greeks, Romans, and Persians were telling a similar story.

The great whale appears in *Pinocchio* too. Remember how the whale swallows Gepetto and Pinocchio? Pinocchio builds a fire inside the whale's belly so the whale spits them out. Natives in Dutch New Guinea tell a similar story! It's an ancient myth that's nearly universal — a whale of a tale.

The whale is what we remember most about the book of Jonah. But that is not what's most important. The great fish is only mentioned in three verses. The whale has only a small walk-on part (or maybe a swim-on part).

So let's not get hooked on the fish! Jonah is no fish story. If I were to sum up the book of Jonah, I'd say it's about second chances, the second chances God gives us, and in most our cases, third and fourth and fifth chances — and also the second chances God asks us to give to each other.

The first second chance we find in the book of Jonah is the second chance God gives Nineveh. The book of Jonah describes Nineveh as "that great city." Like many great cities, past and present, Nineveh saw more than its share of depravity.

It was, as the Bible tells us, a very wicked (Jonah 1:2) and cruel place. The ancient world was cruel. But the Assyrians, located in present-day Iraq, were the cruelest. Modern writers describe them as imperialists, ruthless aggressors, brutal, much feared, and hated.

I am reminded of a line from a poem I learned as a child: "The Assyrian came down like the wolf on the fold, And his cohorts were gleaming in purple and gold" (Lord Byron, "The Destruction of Sennacherib," stanza one). The Assyrians were to their enemies what a wolf is to a sheep. They were not "have a nice day!" smiley face sticker kind of people. Scholars say when Assyria took over Israel, they led their captives back to Mesopotamia with rings pierced through their lips, and chains linking them to another. Can you imagine?

As a group, the Ninevehites were mean and immoral, the Nazi storm troopers of their time. God didn't like it. Didn't like it one bit. He wasn't going to put up with it any longer. We like to stress God's tolerance, God's care, God's compassion, and God's concern. All these are part of God's nature, but that's not the whole story about God.

There are many passages in the Bible that talk clearly about God's judgment. God is a holy God, a righteous God, and a God who gets angry about sin. Jesus gets angry about sin, injustice, and prejudice. In fact, Jesus preaches more about judgment than anyone else in the New Testament except John the Baptist. There is, as a Scottish preacher put it, a "stormy north side to God."

It's always true that "we reap what we sow." Sometimes we "sow our wild oats," then pray for a crop failure! But God's justice will not be mocked (Galatians 6:7). What goes around comes around and evil eventually is punished. Nineveh was cruel, wicked, and offensive — and God was going to drop the hammer on them.

Except... except God gave Nineveh, even evil Nineveh, as bad as toxic waste dumpers, and Afghani car bombers and post-Katrina New Orleans looters, a group of people you and I would write off as hopeless, God gave Nineveh another chance at repentance. God sent Jonah, the prophet, to tell them to shape up.

Jonah didn't want to do it. He hated the Assyrians. His message to Nineveh was gloom and doom. It wasn't easy to hear. He just walked through the city, shouting (probably with satisfaction and delight), "Forty days, and all you creeps will be dead."

Yet, miracle of miracles, Nineveh got the message. Against all odds, Nineveh repented. Go figure! From the king on down, everyone started wearing sackcloth and ashes, praying and fasting. Even the cattle repented! Nineveh put away its wicked ways.

The first second chance in the book of Jonah was extended to Nineveh. The second second chance was for Jonah himself. Jonah was disobedient, disagreeable, prejudiced, bitter, and whiny.

I once heard a little boy, about six years old, in a store, whining about something. His dad said, "I wish I had some cheese to go with that whine!" Jonah was a whiner.

Yet God called Jonah and sent him to Nineveh. Remember how Jonah took off in a boat heading in the opposite direction? How he hid in the hold — as if anyone can hide from God? But God wasn't done with Jonah yet. Remember how God sent a mighty storm at sea to wake him up and shake him up and get his attention? When that didn't work, and Jonah was thrown overboard, remember how God sent a great fish to swallow him and keep him safe?

Remember how Jonah spent three long days in its belly, surrounded by rotting fish and sloshing in digestive juices before he started "blubbering" and came to his senses, gave in, and said he would do what God commanded? Remember how he ended up as fish vomit on the shore? It's not a pretty story.

Jonah remained a complainer. He still hated the Ninevehites. He was quick to point the finger of blame. Jonah reminds me of the minor league baseball coach who was so disgusted with his center fielder's performance that he ordered him to the dugout and took center field himself.

The first ball that came out to center field took a bad hop and hit the coach in the mouth. The next one was a high fly, which he lost in the glare of the sun. It came down and bounced off his forehead! The third one was a hard line drive that he charged after with arms outstretched. It flew between his hands and smacked him in the eye.

Furious, the coach charged back to the dugout, grabbed the center fielder by his uniform, and shouted in his face, "You idiot! You got center field so messed up, even I can't play it!"[1]

Jonah was that kind of person — always attacking, never accepting responsibility. He even blamed God. Still God gives Jonah a second chance. The Bible says, "The word of the Lord came to Jonah a *second* time" with essentially the same message: "Go to Nineveh. Tell them to repent."

The book of Jonah is no fish story. It's about second chances. It's a story written about you and me. Sometimes we're more like Nineveh: wrapped up in dangerous sins, desperately needing to be set free. This reminds me of a tree I once encountered. Behind a parsonage in Massachusetts where we used to live was a maple tree. It was a good-sized tree, tall and healthy. But vines grew thick, as thick as a man's wrist, around that tree. The vines started out small. But they grew fast. Left alone, they would choke the tree. For the good of the tree, the vines had to go. I sawed it off near its roots.

Sin is like that. It starts out small, but it grows fast. Eventually it chokes us. The Ninevehites were wrapped and trapped in sins that were choking them. It was good that God's word of warning came to cut through and set them free. The greatest freedom is not freedom *to* sin but freedom *from* sin. That's why the Ten Commandments, which tell us what to avoid ("Thou shalt not kill, thou shalt not steal, thou shalt not bear false witness, thou shalt not commit adultery.") ought to be renamed "The Ten Freedoms."

No one wants to live in a society where killers, looters, and predators run wild, as they did for a while in New Orleans after Hurricane Katrina, before law and order were restored. Sin running wild isn't freedom. It's terror. Sometimes we are like Nineveh, needing the corrective word of God, the sword of the Lord, which both cuts us and sets us free.

Other times we're more like Jonah: hiding from God, disobedient, self-pitying, quick to point the finger of blame — stop me now if this doesn't sound like you, at least sometimes — complaining, ungiving, unforgiving. Sometimes, like Jonah, we can get so angry with another person that we would almost rather die than forgive them. We hold a grudge like a red-hot coal until it burns us.

Sometimes we're hard as nails, down-and-dirty, sunk-in-sin Nineveh. Other times we're hard-of-hearing and hard-of-heart, like Jonah. No matter who we happen to be at the moment, God always offers us a fresh start, a second chance. Jesus reminds us that God makes the sun to rise on the good and the evil. God sends rain on the just and the unjust. God pays full wages to workers who only start at the end of the day. God throws a party when the prodigal son returns. God is the one who says, to the dying thief, "Today, you will be with me in paradise." God is Jesus, who prays, "Father, forgive them, for they know not what they do" as he hangs on a cross.

The book of Jonah is a wonderful book. I urge you to read it all the way through — maybe later today. You'll find it toward the end of the Old Testament. Jonah is only four chapters. It won't take you long. Read this little book and see if you find yourself in it.

One British author, who read Jonah a hundred times, said that he could never read this book without his pulse beating faster and tears coming to his eyes. He thought it was the greatest book in the Bible.

When you read Jonah, I think you'll find the greatest verse is chapter 4, verse 2: "You are a gracious God, slow to anger, and abounding in steadfast love."

"You are a gracious God, slow to anger, and abounding in steadfast love": a God of second chances, for Nineveh, for Jonah, for you, and for me. A God who expects us to extend second chances to each other. A God who welcomes us here this morning, no matter who we are or how far from God we have traveled.

That's no fish story. It's the very heart of God.

---

1. Ron Hutchcraft, *Wake Up Calls* (Chicago: Moody Press, 1990), p. 46.

Questions for Discussion

1. How are we like Nineveh? How are we like Jonah?

2. Have you ever known what was right and failed to do it anyway?

3. How does God's giving of second chances square with our idea of justice?

4. To whom might you extend a "second chance"? Consider what it might do for both the giver and receiver. Is it, by our standards, *always* wise to offer a second chance?

— Overview —
MICAH

Micah is reminiscent of Amos, whose prophetic ministry came before his. Both were from the Judean countryside. Verse 1:1 names Micah's birthplace as Moresheth. This was a tiny hillside village about 25 miles southwest of Jerusalem. Both men were incensed over social injustice, especially rich and powerful landowners' abuse of the poor. Micah may have been especially sensitized to such injustices, since he was a poor farmer himself. Micah, like Amos, described his enemies with uncompromising frankness. He writes that the rich go to bed "dreaming up crimes... They covet fields and grab them, find homes and take them. They bully the neighbor and his family" (2:1-2 The Message). The religious establishment opposed both Amos and Micah. The priest Amaziah attempted to stifle Amos (Amos 7:10-17). The professional prophets of Jerusalem warned Micah too: " 'Don't preach,' say the preachers. 'Don't preach such stuff. Nothing bad will happen to us. Talk like this to the family of Jacob?' " (2:6-7 The Message).

But there also are differences between Amos and Micah. Amos left Judea to prophesy exclusively against Samaria in the north. Micah preached primarily a coming judgment against his own people in the south, with only a few verses against northern injustices (1:1-7; 6:16). The prologue to Micah indicates he prophesied after Amos, during the reigns of Jotham, Ahaz, and Hezekiah of Judah. Collectively these kings ruled between 750 and 687 BCE. It's unlikely Micah's ministry lasted this entire period — more than six decades. More probable dating would place Micah somewhere between 745 and 710 BCE, making Micah perhaps a generation younger than Amos. But even this is conjecture. Also, Micah's theology is more similar to Hosea's than Amos'. Both Hosea and Micah lift up the Exodus as the supreme sign of God's faithfulness to Israel, making the people's unfaithfulness and apostasy even more marked by contrast.

Micah has inspired at least one hymn: Eric Routley's contemporary "What does the Lord Require?" based on verses 6:1-8.

If one Minor Prophet is preached monthly, Micah falls in April. Earth Day will be on many worshipers' minds — including children, who study it in school. A children's lesson celebrating God's good earth makes a meaningful connection with this sermon. A clear plastic cup of soil might be considered. Dirt seems to be "dead," but it's actually alive with millions of microorganisms, life-enhancing nutrients, and maybe even an earthworm or two. All God's creation is worthy of our respect. We all are called to be stewards of the environment.

What Does the Lord Require?
Micah 6:1-8

Lord F.E. Smith was a noted British barrister active in the early 1900s. Smith once defended a bus company that was being sued. A young man claimed permanent damage to his arm due to the alleged negligence of a bus driver. Smith got the young man on the stand. His cross-examination went something like this.

"Will you please show the court how high you can lift your arm since the accident?" asked Smith. The young man gingerly raised his arm to shoulder level, his face distorted with pain. "Thank you," said Smith. "You may put it down. And now, would you please show the court how high you could lift your arm before the accident?" The young man eagerly shot his arm high above his head and lost the case.

Few of us like to be involved in lawsuits (unless maybe we're lawyers). There's always a danger that the other side may be stronger — or smarter — and win. Yet the passage from Micah, chapter 6, is about a lawsuit. Israel is the Defendant. The prophet is the Prosecutor. The mountains and hills (representing all creation) serve as jury. God almighty is the Plaintiff. The charge against Israel is growing weary of God, of taking God for granted.

Notice, as in many lawsuits, there's an attempt at negotiation. The Defendant, Israel, tries to appease God. Payment in calves and rams and rivers of oil — and maybe even in human beings as religious sacrifices are offered. But God refuses to settle. God is very clear about what God wants from the people. They are to "do justice," "love kindness," and "walk humbly with (their) God."

We all know the expression, "As God is my judge." Well, God *does* judge us. And the Lord's requirements for us are the same three things: that we do justice, that we love kindness, and that we walk humbly with God. How are we doing? Not so well.

I think the jury is out against us. Remember in the Micah passage, the jury was the mountains and the hills. One thing God requires is that we do justice, love kindness, and walk humbly on this planet. And the mountains and hills, rivers and trees condemn us, because we seem to be taking the planet for granted. We're abusing God's good earth.

We all know the grim statistics about the environment. Rain forests are being chopped down to make patio furniture. Every day species wink into extinction, as many and as fast as firefly flashes. In America, 29% of all plant species are threatened. God, who created all things and who loves creation, does have a "bone to pick with us." For you and I have sinned and continue to sin against the earth.

Our sins against the earth are made clear in a litany. It's titled "The Sorrow of the Earth." It begins:

"Listen, my children. The Spirit who moved over the dry land is not pleased. I am thirsty. Are you listening?" The people respond: "We are listening..."

"The Spirit who filled the waters is not pleased. I choke with debris and pollution. Are you listening?" "We are listening, Mother Earth..."

"The Spirit who brought beauty to the earth is not pleased. The earth grows ugly with misuse. Are you listening?" "We are listening..."

"The Spirit who brought forth all the creatures...is not pleased. My creatures are being destroyed. Are you listening?" "We are listening, Mother Earth..."

"The Spirit who gave humans life and a path to walk ...is not pleased. You are losing your humanity and your footsteps stray... Are you listening?" "We are listening..."

That litany sounds like it was written by a close-to-the-earth Native American spiritualist, doesn't it? Or maybe a tree-hugging environmentalist. But it was, in fact, written by a Roman Catholic nun, Sister Mary Rosita Shiosee, S.B.S, and is used in services.[1] The very mountains and hills cry out to us. But... are we listening to the earth?

God requires, God demands that we do justice and love kindness and walk humbly on this planet. So what does it mean to "do justice" to the earth? Perhaps simple justice is valuing the earth not as a thing to use, but for its own intrinsic worth. That is, loving the earth for itself. Genesis 1, verse 31b reads: "God saw everything that (God) had made, and indeed, it was very good." God's creation is good with or without human beings.

Scientists tell us our planet is about five billion years old. That's five thousand million years! For the first four billion, five hundred and ninety-nine million, six hundred thousand years (ninety-nine and nine-tenths of the earth's existence) there were *no* human beings. Civilization and cities only appeared about 10,000 years ago. That's an eye blink in earth's existence.

For the better part of five billion years, the earth got along perfectly well without us. New creatures kept evolving and growing. The earth was drenched in a great tide of life.

Yet in just 200 years since the Industrial Revolution, we humans have begun reversing the tide of life on this planet. We scar the earth and drive thousands of plants and animals into extinction every year.

But, you might be thinking, we are trying to save the whales and the tigers and the giant pandas. That's good. But in God's eyes, each creature, large or small, is precious. In fact, scientists tell us one of the greatest threats to human survival is the rapid extinction of some species of insects. For example, in some areas there has been a dramatic reduction in the number of bees, which we need to pollinate our crops. Plus the whale and the panda and tiger aren't part of our food chain. But insects, eaten by fish, eaten by humans, are. If *they* go, we could too.

So what does it mean to "do justice" to creation? Maybe a good start is simply acknowledging all creation has value. Doing justice might be as simple as trying our best to "live and let live."

If that's "doing justice," then maybe "lovingkindness" is finding better ways to care for God's creation. Besides showing "reverence for life," there are dozens of things we each can do daily to make the earth better — or least not make it worse.

What choices will we make when we decide how warm we will keep our house or apartment in the winter? We can choose to set the thermostat back and wear a sweater. Or how cool we keep our home in the summer? We can turn the air conditioning up, or open a window. In many churches, trustees are replacing thermostats with new, programmable models that save lots of energy. They are putting faceplates on all switches to remind folks to turn off the lights. They are installing up-to-date, energy saving furnaces and storm windows. One church I know of recently put solar panels on its roof.

What choices will we make when it comes to caring for our gardens? Will we just dump on pesticide or learn to live with some bugs? Or search for products that are gentler on the environment?

Loving-kindness is, in part, lifestyle decisions: turning off the lights when leaving a room, remembering to recycle, cutting down on unnecessary travel. Loving-kindness is also about local and national decisions. Like what's the best way to provide power for America? Striving harder to conserve and funding research into alternative energies? Loving-kindness is living more simply. Living simply, so that others, including other creatures, can simply live.

Finally God demands that we walk this earth humbly. That means recognizing our place on this planet as one creature among many. Humankind is not meant to lord it over other kind.

I once read a wonderful illustration of one man walking humbly. A newspaper reporter wrote about a 72-year-old retired executive. He left his house around sunrise three days weekly. He walked two hours out and two hours back on an eight-mile circuit. As he walked, he picked up littered bottles and cans. The man retrieved about 3,500 bottles and cans a year.

Each one was washed out but *not* turned in for the refund. Instead the cleaned bottles and cans were contributed to the Boy and Girl Scouts. Here's a former business executive, giving considerable time and effort every week to clean the environment and support children. I think he typifies the spirit of walking humbly with God.

His walk may not be our walk. But there are things you and I can do. Did you know that every Chinese citizen over the age of eleven, *every* Chinese citizen over the age of eleven, plants three to five trees yearly! They are on their way to reforesting China. You and I can plant trees too. Or contribute to funds that buy up rain forests so that the trees won't be cut down.

The mountains and hills ring out with God's charges against us! Like the people 2,700 years ago, in Micah's day, you and I are on trial! Let us be warned that God has a fearsome love for creation. God loved this earth enough to live on it for a time in a human body. Jesus loved nature enough to speak tenderly about the birds of the air and the lilies of the field. He also took bread and wine, things of the earth, to be symbols of himself. God hears the cries of the earth.

We may be tempted to bargain with God, as

did the Israelites. We may offer calves and rams and rivers of oil. "Take the rest of creation, God, but don't challenge us to change! We may sacrifice the future of our children and grandchildren, their survival on this planet, just so we don't have to change our lifestyles."

But God isn't buying. God has the same three requirements. We are to do justice by respecting creation's integrity. We are to show loving-kindness to the earth through our decisions and actions. We are to walk humbly as one creature among many.

When we do these things, I believe we will be fulfilling God's requirements. And God will work with us and through nature to help restore the planet. Then and only then will we truly walk humbly with God.

---

1. http://www.greenspirit.org.uk/resources/Earthsong.pdf.

Questions for Discussion

1. This scripture has been applied to our contemporary stewardship of the earth. Evaluate the appropriateness of the application.

2. To "do justice" and "loving-kindness" and "walk humbly with (their) God": which do we have the most trouble with? Measure up contemporary American society.

3. Is the litany "The Sorrow of the Earth" consonant with Judeo-Christian teaching? It is certainly consonant with nature worship and other pagan teachings. Where do we agree? Where do we diverge?

4. Examine the concepts: justice versus social justice. How are these terms used today? How will we Christians use them?

5. Discuss the complexity of this ethic of using or abusing our resources and our planet. What of population? We need to be pragmatic about numbers — or do we?

6. What is our responsibility as God's people on this planet? What can we do to walk humbly with our God? Offer ideas.

— Overview —
ZEPHANIAH

Prophets came from a variety of backgrounds. Amos and Micah were farmers. Ezekiel was a priest. Isaiah was of noble birth and served as an advisor to royalty. Verse 1:1 carefully lists Zephaniah's paternal line, going back four generations, probably because his lineage was so distinguished. This prophet was the great-great grandson of King Hezekiah, one of the better kings of Judah. It's likely Zephaniah was a member of the royal court himself during part or all of the 31-year reign of Josiah in Jerusalem.

Zephaniah's prophetic ministry may be dated with some precision. In verse 3:4b he attacks corruption in religious life, declaring Jerusalem's "prophets are reckless, faithless persons; its priests have profaned what is sacred, they have done violence to the law." This best fits a time before Josiah's famous reform, which began in 621 BCE. Verses 2:13-15 predict the fall of Assyria and the destruction of Nineveh, which did not occur until 612 BCE. So Zephaniah likely prophesied sometime early in the reign of Josiah, around 640 to 630 BCE, before either the reform or the fall of Nineveh. It's possible the preaching of his older relative, Zephaniah, was an encouragement to young Josiah's religious reformation, along with the rediscovery of "the book of the law," parts of Deuteronomy, which had been found in the temple (see 2 Kings 22:3ff; 2 Chronicles 34:8ff).

Prominent in Zephaniah are warnings of impending judgment. The day of the Lord is described as a day of terror:

> *(T)he sound of the day of the Lord is bitter, the warrior cries aloud... That day will be a day of wrath, a day of distress and anguish, a day of ruin and devastation, a day of darkness and gloom, a day of clouds and thick darkness, a day of trumpet blast and battle cry.*
> (1:14-16a)

This description is similar to Amos' descriptions of the end times, found in 5:18-20 and 8:9-14. It finds an echo in Matthew 24:29-31.

For Zephaniah the Lord is not just the God of Judah but also the ruler of all nations. Philistia, Moab, Ammon, far-off Ethiopia, and even mighty Assyria stand under God's judgment. Still, this book does not end negatively, but positively, with an explosion of joy. God redeems his people:

> *Sing aloud, O daughter Zion; shout, O Israel! Rejoice and exult with all your heart... The Lord has taken away the judgments against you, he has turned away your enemies. The king of Israel, the Lord is in your midst; you shall fear disaster no more.*
> (3:14-15)

One commentator described this closing scene as a carnival of rejoicing, as God's people sing and dance in their deliverance with the Lord, like a victorious warrior, celebrating along with them.

R.B.Y. Scott's early twentieth-century hymn, "O Day of God, Draw Nigh" fits well with Zephaniah. Scott was a prominent scholar of the Hebrew Scriptures who taught at McGill and Princeton Universities. His book *The Reverence of the Prophets* (London: The McMillan Company, 1973) remains a helpful introduction to Hebrew prophesy.

Swiss developmental psychologist Jean Piaget famously labeled the years five through nine of childhood as the stage of moral realism. Youngsters this age are focused on the consequences of actions. So they relate easily to the Golden Rule, as found in Matthew 7:12.

An appropriate children's lesson might focus on what adults call the ethics of reciprocity. If we don't want to get picked on, we shouldn't pick on others. If we don't want gossip spread about us, we should not spread tales about others. Similarly, if children want to be treated kindly, they must treat others the same. It's the Golden Rule, which always and inevitably works.

What Goes Around, Comes Around: God Is Not Mocked
Zephaniah 3:14-18a

Clive Staples Lewis, C.S. Lewis, is well known for his *Chronicles of Narnia* allegorical children's stories. Three of them, *The Lion, the Witch and the Wardrobe*; *Prince Caspian*; and *The Voyage of the Dawn Treader* have been made into movies. Maybe you also saw the film about Lewis' life, *Shadowlands*, starring Anthony Hopkins and Debra Winger. C.S. Lewis was a major figure in the twentieth century. Some describe him as one of the 100 most influential writers to live in those 100 years.

One way he was important was his demand we get back to basics. Lewis called for a return to time-honored values. He spoke strongly against moral relativism. It's not true, he said, that it's "different strokes for different folks," "No harm, no foul." He didn't believe in "have it your way Burger King ethics," where nothing is right or wrong anymore. It's just what you feel.

No, Lewis insisted there are universal laws — lots of them. For example, consider a list found in the appendix of one of his books, *The Abolition of Man*. It is dozens of illustrations of what Lewis labels the Tao, or natural law. These are moral principals found in every society in history, ethical ideas we dare not ignore.

For example, "Do unto others as you would have them do unto you." That's how Jesus put it (Matthew 7:12). But ancient Babylonians, living 1,500 years before Christ had something similar to say in one of their hymns: "Speak kindness (to others)... show good will."

Five hundred years before Jesus, Confucius wrote in China, "He whose heart is in the smallest degree set on goodness will dislike no one." Cicero, a Roman living about fifty years before Jesus, said, "Men were brought into existence for (others) that they might do one another good." That's the Golden Rule, stated in four different ways in four different societies, at four different periods. Looking out for your neighbor is a universal law.

Lewis' "everywhere/anytime" morality includes laws demanding we show special concern for our parents, plus laws about truth-telling, sexual purity, and honest testimony in court. (Does this sound at all like the Ten Commandments?) By calling us back to universal values, Lewis was a prophet crying against the moral laxity of his time. "Yes," said Lewis, "there are rules, universal ones, and we must honor and keep them."

The law undergirding all the other laws is the Law of Consequences or the Law of Cause and Effect. It's captured in common sayings, "What goes around, comes around"; "You get back what you give"; "You reap what you sow." The last is from the Bible. It's found in Galatians: "Do not be deceived; God is not mocked, for you reap whatever you sow" (6:7). Eastern religions call this balance "karma."

The point is, no one gets away with evil scot-free. Eventually the wrong we do comes back to haunt us. Rest assured, we do pay.

Twenty-six hundred years before C.S. Lewis, another prophet had a similar message. Some of what Zephaniah said, no doubt, was pretty popular in his day. He applied the law of "what goes around, comes around" to the nations that surrounded his little country of Judea. Zephaniah had harsh words for the Philistines, the seagoing people who lived to the west. "Ah, you inhabitants of the seacoast... The word of the Lord is against you... land of the Philistines; and I will destroy you until no inhabitant is left" (2:5). I can picture Zephaniah's Jewish hearers nodding their heads and smiling in agreement. "We hate those Philistines!"

He goes on to attack Moab and Ammon, two other small, nearby nations. They've taunted God's people, and you reap what you sow: "Moab shall become like Sodom and the Ammonites like Gomorrah" (2:9b). The crowd likes this too. "Preach it, brother. Burn 'em up like Sodom and Gomorrah!"

Zephaniah gives a side-glance to the Ethiopians, who are far away, and condemns them. The Lord says, they "shall be killed by my sword" (2:12). This is getting better and better. Zephaniah has the crowd eating out of his hand. He takes on the biggest bully on the block, the bloodthirsty Assyrians, the Nazi storm troopers in their time, who were threatening little Judea. The angry prophet proclaims,

> (The Lord) will stretch out his hand... and destroy Assyria... he will make Nineveh (its capital) a desolation, a dry waste like the desert. Herds shall lie down in it, every wild animal; the desert owl and screech owl shall lodge in its capitals; the owl shall hoot at the window, the raven croak on the threshold.
> (2:13-14)

(the owl and raven were considered unclean birds, not fit to eat). Zephaniah continues,

> Is this the exultant city that lived secure, that said... "I am, and there is no one else"? What a desolation it has become, a lair for wild animals! Everyone who passes by hisses and shakes (his) fist.
> (2:15)

The crowd goes wild! "That's right, Lord! Pile a heap of hurting on Nineveh. They push us around. Beat 'em with an ugly stick!"

In art, Zephaniah is always pictured as the prophet holding a lamp. It's not the warm glow of a friendly candle, but the searing beam of a searchlight that exposes dirt and flaws. His words are urgent, fierce, and demanding. Now he turns the spotlight of God's judgment on Jerusalem. What goes around, comes around applies to his people, too:

> Ah, soiled, defiled, and oppressing city! (Jerusalem, you) have listened to no voice... have accepted no correction. (You) have not trusted in the Lord... (your) officials are roaring lions; (your) judges are (a pack of ravenous) wolves... (your) priests have profaned what is

> sacred, they have done violence to the law...
> the unjust knows no shame.
> (3:1-5)

The crowd grew quiet. Zephaniah was warning that God was about to drop the hammer on God's own people. The Law of Consequences applies to them too. God's law is ironclad, and God is not mocked. We reap what we sow. As Hosea put it, Israel had sown the wind. So they will reap the whirlwind of God's anger. They plowed wickedness and will harvest a crop of injustice (Hosea 8:7; 10:13).

Of the twelve Minor Prophets, Zephaniah may be the darkest. Someone suggested he must have been "baptized in vinegar." That's why so few preachers preach on him. His message is almost totally gloom and doom.

Remarkably, this "scandal in sandals," who boldly attacked the people and their leaders and held them accountable, was not a member of the underclass, oppressed by injustice. No, Zephaniah was a member of the royal household itself, one of the privileged few! One commentator calls him a prince. His great-great grandfather was Hezekiah, one of the better kings, who, in his own way, was a religious reformer. Yet Zephaniah, speaking for the Lord, proclaimed, "I will punish the officials and the king's sons..." (1:8b).

Like C.S. Lewis in our time, Zephaniah wanted people in his time to get back to basics — to honor and obey the laws of God that were created for their good. Complacency, pride, and haughtiness were rejected; humility and lowliness sought; lying, cheating, and deceit denied. Only when they changed their hearts and their ways would God call back punishment. Then the repentant people will "pasture and lie down, and no one will make them afraid" (see 1:12b; 3:11-13).

I once preached a series on the Ten Commandments, twelve sermons in all, one commandment a month, with an introduction and conclusion. These ten guidelines for godly living are timeless. C.S. Lewis would label them the Tao, universal Law.

God says:

> *Thou shalt have no other Gods before me.*
> *Thou shalt not make unto thee any graven image.*
> *Thou shalt not take the name of the Lord thy God in vain.*
> *Remember the Sabbath day, to keep it holy.*
> *Honor thy father and thy mother.*
> *Thou shalt not kill.*
> *Thou shalt not commit adultery.*
> *Thou shalt not steal.*
> *Thou shalt not bear false witness against thy neighbor.*
> *Thou shalt not covet thy neighbor's house, thou shalt not covet thy neighbor's wife, nor his manservant, nor his ox, nor his (donkey), nor anything that is thy neighbor's.*
> (Exodus 20:1-17 RSV)

God created the universe to run on laws, like the law of gravity. If you jump off a ten-story building, you don't break the law of gravity. It breaks you. Likewise God gave the Ten Commandments as moral guidelines. When we break them, we do so at our peril. In the process, we break our relationship with God, destroy community, and break ourselves. Pain and suffering result.

Prophets like C.S. Lewis and Zephaniah must be taken seriously, by individuals and by nations. It's worth asking, "Is America living up to God's high standards?" "Is there economic, social, and political justice?" "Is God worshiped rightly here?" "Do our leaders lead well?" "What do you think?" "How pleased is God with us?"

What goes around, comes around. God is not mocked. God's high standards apply to us as individuals and to our much-favored nation.

God's judgment — the day of the Lord — is serious business. It's supposed to be scary. Sometimes we need to be "scared straight," straight back to the Ten Commandments. But judgment is hopeful too, if it leads to repentance and the amendment of life.

There was a revival in Zephaniah's time when an old, forgotten Book of the Law, Deuteronomy, was rediscovered and the prophet's harsh words were heard and heeded. Under King Josiah, Zephaniah's relative, Judah underwent a religious reform starting from the top down.

The king tore his clothes, a gesture of despair. He ordered the temple and temple worship cleaned up. Practices like child sacrifice and temple prostitution, ugly in themselves, which break the Ten Commandments, were rejected. The Passover, celebrating God's power and goodness in the Exodus, was brought back after years of neglect.

The result: Judah escaped God's fierce judgment. For a time, the people lived at peace. There was a carnival of joy. Part of Zephaniah's final vision, the only upbeat verses in his book, was lived out:

> *Sing... O daughter of Zion... Rejoice and exult with all your heart... The Lord has taken away the judgments against you... The king of Israel, the Lord, is in your midst... The Lord, your God, is... a warrior who gives victory; He will rejoice over you with gladness, he will renew you in his love; he will exult over you with loud singing as on a day of festival.*
> (3:14-18a)

There was rejoicing, because the people were right again with God.

It's God's nature to judge. God is holy. Holiness hates sin, the way a mother hates the disease that would take her child's life. We are under God's judgment. But God is not judgment. Scripture doesn't say "God is judgment." It says "God is love" (1 John 4:8). The kind of fatherly love that welcomes back the prodigal who comes to his senses, the sort of good shepherding love that seeks lost sheep. God's love is seen supremely in Christ's self-sacrifice for us on the cross.

When we turn back to God and God's law, God rejoices over us and renews us. Yes, what goes around comes around. Yes, we get back what we give. Yes, God is not mocked. We reap what we sow.

But thank God that's not the last word. God shows mercy when we repent and turn back to him. So said C.S. Lewis. So said Zephaniah (3:17b). So says the gospel: "If we confess our sins, he who is faithful and just will forgive us our sins and cleanse us from all unrighteousness" (1 John 1:9). That's always good news.

Questions for Discussion

1. How do the Ten Commandments work for us today? Which are in our laws? Which are embedded in our societal expectations? Why are these commandments banned in public places in American society today?

2. On what basis do we imagine we are the people of God? What is expected of us?

3. Where is Christianity growing? Where is God speaking and advancing?

4. Where shall we judge others? Where shall we not?

5. Are there other quotes from C.S. Lewis that would enrich our discussion?

— Overview —
NAHUM

This prophet is something of a mystery. Verse 1:1 tells us Nahum was from Elkosh, likely a small town or village, which remains unidentified. Unlike Hosea, Jonah, Micah, and Zephaniah, scripture provides no information about this prophet's family. His name means "consolation." This is ironic, since his message to Nineveh was far from comforting. Nahum's vivid descriptions of Nineveh cause some scholars to speculate he knew that city well, either as a visitor or perhaps as a resident. Nahum might even have been the descendant of Israelite exiles who settled in Nineveh after 721 BCE. But this is supposition.

It appears fairly easy to date his book. Verses 3:8-10 mention the destruction of the Egyptian city of Thebes by the Assyrians. This took place in 663 BCE. Nahum predicts the fall of Nineveh. The Assyrian capitol fell to a coalition of the Babylonians, Medes, and Scythians in 612 BCE. So it's likely this prophet preached against Nineveh in the half century between 663 and 612 BCE.

Most of Nahum is striking poetry. Chapter 1 may be an alphabetic poem, like Psalms 110, 111, 118, and 145, where each line begins with a successive letter of the Hebrew alphabet. Chapters 2 and 3 likewise are a poem, or poems, notable for their imagery. The language is terse and powerful. For example, verse 2:1, in Hebrew would read something like "Ramparts guarded! Road watched! Loins girded! Strength collected!" in which the articles dropped for maximum affect. Scholars label these passages taunt songs, similar in character to Isaiah 46 and 47, where an enemy is goaded and derided. Nahum rejoices in the city's pending destruction, when bodies will be stacked, one upon the other, like cordwood.

This causes some commentators theological problems. Questions are raised about why Nahum is included in the canon at all. Christians are taught to love their enemies and to pray for their persecutors (Matthew 5:44). Where's the good news in the burning and looting of an entire city and the slaughter of its inhabitants?

Still, God's judgment and mercy are two sides of the same coin. Would we want to live in a world where wickedness and sin, like that of cruel Nineveh, went unpunished? Scattered through the first chapter of Nahum are hopeful verses, such as "the Lord is slow to anger, but great in power" (v. 3a) and "Look! On the mountains the feet of one who brings good tidings, who proclaims peace" (v. 15a). The latter is echoed in Isaiah 52:7. So, yes, God is "a jealous and avenging God... The mountains quake before him, and the hills melt... His wrath is poured out like fire" (1:2, 5-6). But also "The Lord is good, a stronghold in a day of trouble; he protects those who take refuge in him, even in a rushing flood" (1:7-8a).

Two hymns fit Nahum well. Both remind us of the frailty of human power and hubris "Not Alone for Mighty Empire" and "O Where Are Kings and Empires Now?"

A children's lesson could focus on the Pledge of Allegiance to the Flag, which proclaims America is "one nation, under God." The motto "in God we trust," on all our coins and paper currency could be shown. Children might be asked what it means to put ourselves "under God" and to proclaim we trust "in God." The point could be made that ultimately it's not reliance on armies, navies, or air forces that keeps a nation strong. It's obedience to and reliance on God that's the source of security and strength.

Lest We Forget
Nahum 1:2-7

This is halfway through our series on the Not-So-Minor Prophets. There are twelve, and I number Nahum as sixth chronologically. What can we say about Nahum that's meaningful for today? I tried several different approaches to this sermon.

It might be interesting to compare and contrast Nahum with Jonah. After all, both prophets preached to Nineveh, by my reckoning, about a hundred years apart. That's a similarity. Jonah and Nahum both end on questions. Another similarity.

But there are differences between these two as well. In Jonah, it's the prophet who's disobedient and Nineveh that's obedient. Remember how Jonah tried to escape God by sailing in the other direction? But wicked Nineveh, surprisingly, obeyed God and was spared?

Nahum reverses this. In Nahum, the prophet is faithful, but Nineveh remains unrepentant. In Jonah, the city is saved. In Nahum, it's destroyed.

Jonah, the prophet, was rescued *from* water. In the midst of a storm, a great fish swallowed Jonah whole, then spat him out on land three days later. In Nahum, nasty Nineveh was destroyed *by* water. In 612 BCE, there was a flood, which some commentators say the prophet predicted (2:6). A river running through the city overflowed, wiping out a defensive wall. Nineveh's enemies swept in, looting and killing.

Which brings up another approach to Nahum, which I also considered. This book is astonishing poetry. It has been called world literature. The images of Nineveh's destruction are powerful and disturbing. Nahum writes,

> *A shatterer has come up against you. Guard the ramparts; watch the road; gird your loins; collect all your strength... The shields of his warriors are red; his soldiers are clothed in crimson. The metal on the chariots flashes... the chargers prance. The chariots race madly through the streets, they rush to and fro through the squares; their appearance is like torches, they dart like lightning.*
> (2:1-4)

Can't you picture the bloodthirsty warriors rampaging through the city?

> *The crack of whip and rumble of wheel, galloping horse and bounding chariot! Horsemen charging, flashing sword and glittering spear, piles of dead, heaps of corpses, dead bodies without end — they stumble over the bodies!*
> (3:2-3)

That's as good a description of ancient warfare as ever written anywhere! Nahum reminds us much of the Bible is poetic. A sermon — or several — could be preached on poetry in God's word, starting here.

Another sermon might describe ancient Nineveh and why it deserved God's judgment.

This city was, as Nahum put it, a "city of bloodshed, utterly deceitful, full of booty — (with) no end to plunder" (3:1). To everyone else in the ancient world, the Assyrians were what a wolf is to sheep. Remember Lord Byron's poem, "The Assyrian came down like the wolf on the fold, And his cohorts were gleaming in purple and gold"? The Assyrians were like a pack of wolves, destroying and devouring weaker nations.

So those are three possible sermons. But none explains what Nahum has to do with us today. What *does* a prophecy about the downfall of a long-forgotten kingdom have to say to you and me today?

As best as I can determine, the book of Nahum is a warning. In its time, Assyria was a superpower. Today America is the only superpower left. In spite of the Great Recession, the worst economic down turn in over 25 years, despite troops in Afghanistan and Iraq, in spite of bankrupt banks, and once-bankrupt General Motors and Chrysler, despite the lingering threat of terrorism, in spite of it all, no other nation has the power and might to stand against America.

America remains number one. But that brings dangers. Remember that "the bigger they are, the harder they fall."

Some present-day prophets urgently point out the threat in our position. I think of Andrew Bacevich, who wrote the bestseller, *The Limits of Power*. Its subtitle is sobering: *The End of American Exceptionalism*. Bacevich is a Princeton Ph.D. who teaches history and international relations at Boston University. His book is a critique of our country, on three important fronts.

By the way, let me say, before someone writes him off, Bacevich is no "bleeding heart Liberal." He's a self-described Conservative, West Point graduate, and retired Army Colonel, who did a tour in Vietnam. This book is dedicated to his son, Andrew, another West Point grad, who was killed in Iraq. Bacevich is a patriot who loves America. That's why he's worried about us.

The author sees this as a dangerous time for our country. The threat is not out there but internal. One issue he focuses on at length is our national addiction to and craving for more and more, captured by the bumper stickers "Whoever dies with the most toys, wins"; "Shop till you drop"; "If it feels good, do it."[1] We've changed from an ethic of self-sacrifice to an ethic of self-gratification, from a nation of producers to a nation of consumers. In the process, we've allowed ourselves to get hooked on cheap Chinese goods and Middle Eastern oil.

Bacevich writes, "Just as the lunch-bucket-toting factory worker had symbolized the empire of production... the teenager, daddy's credit card in her blue jeans and headed to the mall, now has emerged as the empire of consumption's emblematic figure."[2] This addiction to consumption makes us vulnerable, militarily and economically, to often-hostile forces beyond our borders. America is weakened by our refusal to keep our appetites in check and live within our means.

This crisis of overspending is tied to a political crisis. Bacevich writes, "American political leaders — especially at the national level — have proven unable (or unwilling) to address the disparity between how much (Americans) want and what we can afford... Successive administrations, abetted by Congress, have deepened a looming crisis of debt and dependency through unbridled spending.[3] Often excess spending is justified in the name of national security, which demands ever-larger defense budgets.[4] The failure of politicians to live within America's means falls on both parties," Bacevich states.[5]

According to Bacevich, the third issue that threatens our security is a misguided belief that armies, air forces, and navies alone can defend us. Bacevich isn't a pacifist. He knows it's a dangerous world. But he also recognizes the limits of power. He writes, "(T)he United States is ill-prepared to fight a global war (on terror) with no exits and no deadlines. The sole superpower lacks the resources — economic, political, and military, to support a large-scale, protracted conflict without, at the very least, inflicting severe economic and political damage on itself."[6]

He notes the burden of fighting in Afghanistan and Iraq is being borne by a smaller and smaller percentage of our society, mostly "rural Americans, people of color, recent immigrants, and members of the working class."[7] They often are ordered back to the war zone for multiple tours of duty that get longer and longer, while the rest of us sacrifice little. Is that fair?

Bacevich often quotes Reinhold Niebuhr, another prophet from the 1950s and '60s. You may know Niebuhr as the author of the famous Serenity Prayer. Less well known is Reinhold and his brother, H. Richard, considered two of the three greatest native-born American theologians. (Jonathan Edwards, the great preacher and evangelist from the eighteenth century, is the third. All three are from the UCC tradition).[8]

A half-century ago, Niebuhr warned "the American nation has become strangely enamored with military might" and warned against developing dangerous delusions about ourselves, our goodness, and our power. Niebuhr wrote, "Every nation has its own form of spiritual pride." Every nation believes it's special, even exceptional and God-favored. But, as Bacevich notes, "(W)e do not differ from other great powers as much as we imagine."[9]

The most dangerous sin is pride Niebuhr often stated. He called it "hubris." Because, as Proverbs reminds us, "Pride goes... before a fall" (16:18 RSV). If we, as a nation, don't recognize the limits of our power — that we're not indispensable to the world, that we can't fix everyone's problems — if we don't recognize our limitations, both economic and military and live within them, we, too could fall. Ancient Assyria did.

That's the message I get from Nahum. It's a warning to every great power, like ours. As Nahum reminds us, God is a jealous God who does not suffer anyone or anything as a rival. We must not put anything, even our nation, ahead of God. Those nations that survive and thrive recognize themselves, as the Pledge of Allegiance puts it, as being "under God."

Rudyard Kipling said this well in a poem from the nineteenth century. Kipling is well known as the author of children's books like *The Jungle Book* and *Just So Stories*, and popular novels like *Kim*. He was a great champion of the British empire, which in his day, was the strongest power on earth. Kipling was so nationalistic that George Orwell, the novelist, labeled him "the poet of British imperialism." Kipling popularized the phrase "The White Man's Burden."

Yet he also recognized the limits of power and that his great nation needed to subject itself to God. Consider his poem "Recessional," which he wrote for national holiday:

> God of our fathers, known of old,
>   Lord of our far-flung battle-line,
> Beneath whose awful Hand we hold
>   Dominion over palm and pine —
> Lord God of Hosts, be with us yet,
> Lest we forget — lest we forget!
>
> The tumult and the shouting dies;
>   The Captains and the Kings depart;
> Still stands Thine ancient sacrifice,
>   An humble and a contrite heart.
> Lord God of Hosts, be with us yet,
> Lest we forget — lest we forget!
>
> Far-called, our navies melt away;
>   On dune and headland sinks the fire:
> Lo, all our pomp of yesterday
>   Is one with Nineveh and Tyre!
> Judge of the Nations, spare us yet,
> Lest we forget — lest we forget!
>
> If drunk with sight of power, we loose
>   Wild tongues that have not Thee in awe,
> Such boastings as the Gentiles use,
>   Or lesser breeds without the Law —
> Lord God of Hosts, be with us yet,
> Lest we forget — lest we forget!
>
> For heathen heart that puts her trust
>   In reeking tube and iron shard,
> All valiant dust that builds on dust,

> And guarding, calls not Thee to guard,
> For frantic boast and foolish word —
> Thy mercy on Thy People, Lord![10]

The poet is praying his nation — then the most powerful on earth — not lose its perspective. Kipling knew that armies and navies alone cannot keep us safe. Rather it's faith in God and obedience to God's will that makes a nation strong.

The bad news is "a jealous and avenging God is the Lord, the Lord is avenging and wrathful; the Lord takes vengeance on his adversaries and rages against his enemies," as Nahum put it (v. 2). God will suffer no rivals. Human pride and self-righteousness, either individual or national, will not stand against God.

The good news is "the Lord is slow to anger..." and "the Lord is good, a stronghold in a day of trouble; he protects those who take refuge in him..." (Nahum 1:2-3a, 7). Prophets, like Nahum, Bacevich, Niebuhr, and Kipling have been saying so for centuries. Lord God of hosts, be with us yet, lest we forget, lest we forget!

---

1. Quotes from *The Limits of Power: The End of American Exceptionalism* by Andrew J. Bacevich. Copyright © 2008 by Andrew J. Bacevich. Reprinted by permission of Henry Holt and Company, LLC.
2. *Ibid.*, p. 29.
3. *Ibid.*, p. 10.
4. *Ibid.*, pp. 72, 82-83.
5. *Ibid.*, p. 70.
6. *Ibid.*, p. 11.
7. *Ibid.*, p. 140.
8. Edwards was a Congregationalist. The Niebuhrs were Evangelical and Reformed. The Congregational Christian and Evangelical

and Reformed denominations merged to form the United Church of Christ in 1957.

9. Andrew J. Bacevich, Boston University Lecture, October 9, 2007, found online at http://www.pbs.org/moyers/journal/08/15/2008/profilee.html.

10. Rudyard Kipling, "Recessional," http://wikipedia.com.

Questions for Discussion

1. In your estimation, why is Nahum included in the canon?

2. Is a God of judgment and a God of mercy at odds?

3. Many classrooms today forgo the Pledge of Allegiance, as "in God we trust" is a bone of contention. How do these traditional patriotic phrases face challenges today? Does God belong in school today?

4. Compare Jonah and Nahum. They both end in questions. Do they answer the questions they pose?

5. Evaluate the book of Nahum as poetry.

6. As warning, what does Nahum have for us to learn?

7. What, if anything, does Bacevich add to our conversation? Do you agree with him?

8. It is dangerous to connect God with the triumphs (and failures) of our side. How can we be assured that God is "on our side"?

— Overview —
OBADIAH

Verse 1 tells us the book of Obadiah resulted from a vision. The prophet foresaw God's coming judgment on Edom. This small nation, located directly to the south of Judea, had cooperated with the Babylonians in pillaging and destroying Jerusalem in 587 BCE. The sacking of the city is described graphically in verses 10-15.

Edom's complicity in the devastation was especially painful for the Judeans; first because the Edomites were their close neighbors, second because Edom and Judah were understood to be related. Both were Semitic peoples. Genesis traces each back to a common ancestor, the patriarch Isaac. Tradition held that the Judeans developed from the line of Isaac's son, Jacob/Israel, and the Edomites from his twin brother Esau (see Genesis 36:9).

Obadiah's bitterness over Edom's betrayal is evident. Verse 10 states: "For the slaughter and violence done to *your brother* Jacob, shame shall cover you, and you shall be cut off forever." Verse 12a reads: "(Y)ou should not have gloated over your *brother* on the day of his misfortune..." (emphasis added). Edom's vicious attack was harder to bear because a neighbor and "brother" proved to be an enemy. Obadiah reveled in his vision of

Edom's pending destruction. The Edomites (temporarily) were soaring like an eagle, but God would bring them down (v. 4). God surely would make them "the least among the nations." They will be "utterly despised," predicted Obadiah (v. 2).

Some dismiss this book as a bitter, nationalistic outburst. But as one commentator notes, there is a major message in this minor prophet. Good news comes in verses 17-21, with Obadiah's vision of Judah's restoration and the coming day of the Lord. The exiles will return. Mount Zion again will be holy and "the kingdom shall be the Lord's." God will reign and there will be justice. This is a vision believers can cling to in difficult times.

Hymns related to Obadiah include "God of Our Fathers," "Whose Almighty Hand," and Lloyd Stone's 1934 hymn, "This Is My Song," especially including his original third verse, which is missing from many hymnals:

> *May truth and freedom come to every nation;*
> *May peace abound where strife has raged so long,*
> *That each may seek to love and build together*
> *A world united, righting every wrong —*
> *A world united in its love for freedom,*
> *Proclaiming peace together in one song.*

That's a vision of brotherhood and sisterhood in action!

Sibling rivalry is a topic most children will understand. It's covered in two titles from the Berenstain Bears series. Both *The Berenstain Bears*

Get in a Fight (New York: Random House, 1982) and *The Berenstain Bears Hug and Make Up* (New York: Harper Festival, 2006) address this subject. Either is short enough to read with the youngsters as a children's lesson. These particular titles are not overtly religious, but the entire series is informed by the Berenstains' evangelical faith.

When Families Fight
Obadiah 10-15

There are 66 books in the Protestant version of the Bible. Obadiah is one of the shortest. It's the smallest book in the Old Testament. Only Second and Third John in the New Testament have fewer verses. Still, there are major messages in this Minor Prophet.

One is the theme we got from Zephaniah: What goes around, comes around. God is not mocked. The Edomites mistreated the Judeans, God's chosen people, their neighbors to the north. In 587 BCE, Edom joined Babylon in attacking and sacking Jerusalem. Between them, Babylon and Edom destroyed the city. Then the Babylonians deported much of the population.

Obadiah the prophet predicted the end of aggressor Edom: "(T)he day of the Lord is near... As you have done, it shall be done to you; your deeds will return on your own head" (v. 15). Or as The Message Bible puts it, "What you did will boomerang back."

God is judge of all nations and punishes wickedness whenever and wherever it arises. Obadiah was confident Edom would "get theirs." In God's good time, Israel would be restored. Which is what happened. It took years, but ancient Edom is gone now, while a revived Israel continues. What goes around comes around and God is not mocked.

For me, another message from this book is the danger of family fights. Edom's betrayal of Israel was more painful because the two nations were understood as related. The Bible traces these two peoples back to one set of parents: Isaac and Rebekah.

You might remember they had twin boys. The elder twin was Esau. He grew up a sunburned, hairy man, a great outdoors man and wonderful hunter. Esau was impulsive but still his father's favorite. Isaac loved the wild game stew Esau made. The younger twin was Jacob, cunning and crafty. Jacob was the "momma's boy" favored by Rebekah.

Their rivalry began before they were born. Genesis says they struggled in the womb.

When they came out, the younger grabbed the heel of the firstborn, as if to pull him back (Genesis 25:26). Later, Jacob talked his brother out of his inheritance (Genesis 25:33) and stole his father's blessing. Esau got so angry he decided to murder Jacob. His brother ran away from home and stayed away for years (Genesis 27).

A family fight: rival brothers, each threatening or abusing the other; two parents at odds, both playing favorites. According to the Bible, the two brothers gave rise to two nations. Esau was the father of Edom. (It's interesting Edom was a land of red, sandy cliffs and Esau is depicted as "red-faced.") Jacob became the father of Israel.

The Bible uses the tension between these two to explain tensions between the two nations for a thousand years. When Moses asked permission for the Israelites to pass through Edom into the

Promised Land after the Exodus centuries later, the Edomites refused (Numbers 20:14-21). Later the kings of Israel attacked and subjugated Edom many times, starting with Saul (1 Samuel 14:47). Rivalry between these related peoples went on for the better part of a millennium. To me, it's as if scripture was saying, "There can be long-term consequences to family fights."

Some of the most painful situations pastors encounter are family fights. One example: two sisters lived in the same tiny town. They hadn't spoken in years. In their community there was one small post office and few stores. But if they met getting the mail or on the street, both turned away without speaking.

One made the other angry by something she did on her sister's wedding day. When it came time to cut the cake, she went ahead and cut slices of her sister's wedding cake, and passed them out, without first asking permission. Words were exchanged and the two sisters couldn't forgive what happened decades before. They never spoke again — not a word — before one died.

A pastor visited one of the sisters who was in the hospital as she was dying. She made the pastor promise not to tell her sister about her condition, lest the sister visit her in the hospital, and make up. In fact, she made sure there was no death notice in the paper or word about her funeral until after she was buried. That way her sister couldn't attend her calling hours or funeral! She took her bitterness to the grave. Sad, but true.

When families fight, things can get ugly, can't they? What do families fight about? Who loves Dad or Mom more or who does more for them.

Who does Dad or Mom love more. What sister Sylvia said to brother Bob ten years ago at the family reunion. Keepsakes. Property. Possessions. Money. You name it.

Families are supposed to be blessings. Smart people say so. Author Alex Haley wrote, "(T)he family is link to the past, bridge to the future." Historian Will Durant said, "The family is the nucleus of civilization." Philosopher and playwright George Bernard Shaw wrote, "A happy family is but an earlier heaven." Another philosopher, George Santayana said, "The family is one of nature's masterpieces."

However, sometimes families can be places of pain and not pleasure, can't they? Scripture knows this well. The Bible is filled with family fights. Some biblical families were so dysfunctional they make ours look like a picnic. Adam blamed Eve for eating the apple (Genesis 3:12). Cain murdered his brother, Abel (Genesis 4:8). Amnon lusted after, then sexually assaulted his stepsister, Tamar. Her biological brother killed him in revenge (2 Samuel 13). King David's favorite son, Absalom, tried to steal the kingdom from his father (2 Samuel 15), and so on.

Family fights hurt us. I suspect they hurt God. For example, what about family fights between the children of Abraham? For me, these too are symbolized in the book of Obadiah. Genesis says Abraham, grandfather of Jacob and Esau, was the father of all Jews (Genesis 12:2). Jews and Christians, of course, are related so Christians look back to Abraham too. Muslims believe Abraham, through another son, Ishmael, was the father of Islam. Jews, Christians, and Muslims are "Abrahamic religions." All three trace back to Abraham. We worship the same God. Scholars speak of a Judeo-Christian-Islamic tradition. We could — and should — be a loving family of religions.

But some Jews persecuted the earliest Christians. Some Christians persecuted Jews for centuries in Europe. Christians launched Crusades against Islam. Muslims have fought both Jews and Christians. Now Jews and Muslims battle over the Holy Land.

Most parents are unhappy to see their children fight, aren't they? I wonder if fighting between God's children wounds God? Could God be especially saddened when religion is used as a weapon to attack, destroy, maim, and kill?

Family fights can get out of hand, can't they? How to stop them? Here are a few thoughts about healing. They're gleaned from the reading I've done, as well as my own reflections on this problem over the decades.

First, if we're in a family fight, we need to maintain our perspective. Sometimes we think we're the only one who's right, and the other is totally wrong. But things are rarely that simple.

In a family fight, a little humility goes a long way toward healing. Saint Paul reminds us in 2 Corinthians that we're all "clay pots." What's a clay pot? In Paul's day it was a humble, common, ordinary vessel. In Romans he notes, "All have sinned and fall short of the glory of God" (3:23). He echoes the Hebrew Scriptures, saying, "None is righteous, no not one" (Romans 3:10 RSV). We're all clay pots. All of us are sinners. None of us is utterly blameless.

Some clay pots are bigger than others. Some are stronger. Some are better looking. But in the end they're the same: fragile, breakable, common clay. Before we get on a high horse and put down a family member, can we take a moment to review our shortcomings, and see what we might have contributed to the problem? No one is completely righteous, no, not one.

Second, in a family fight, hard as it is, try to stay connected. Family fights feed off poor communication. Write letters or send emails. Let your estranged family member know you're well. Share good news like graduations or the birth of a baby but don't gloat. Stay in touch with family members they're close to as well. Avoid the temptation to get others to take your side.

Ephesians advises us,

> Let no evil talk come out of your mouths, but only what is useful for building up... Put away from you all bitterness and wrath and anger and wrangling and slander, together with all malice, and be kind to one another, tenderhearted, forgiving one another, as God in Christ has forgiven you.
> (4:29, 31-32)

Third, enlist the help of non-involved family members. Family fights affect the whole family. So stay in touch with others your estranged family members are close to. They can pass messages for you. "How wonderful, how beautiful, when brothers and sisters get along!" the Psalmist says (133:1 The Message).

Be the first to take a step toward reconciliation. Call up the family member with whom you are fighting and invite him or her to dinner, maybe in a public place, where voices are less likely to be raised.

Jesus tells us we must be the first to reach out to an estranged sister or brother, difficult as that is:

> *(W)hen you are offering your gift at the altar, if you remember that your brother or sister has something against you, leave your gift there before the altar and go; first be reconciled with your brother or sister, then come and offer your gift.*
> (Matthew 5:23-24)

Finally, try to set realistic expectations. The aim is to reestablish a level of reconciliation, rather than resolve every old disagreement or slight. This in itself may take considerable effort. A goal might simply be to spend time together around a holiday without an argument erupting. Family fights are painful but with God's help, they can be resolved. As Luke puts it, "Nothing will be impossible with God" (3:47).

What can we do about that big family fight between Jews, Christians, and Muslims? If I could solve that, I'd be Secretary General of the UN! But I can tell you what one institution is doing. Andover Newton Theological School has taken a lead in Jewish/Christian/Muslim reconciliation. It shares a hilltop outside Boston with Hebrew College, a Jewish institution. They swap professors and offer joint classes. Students attend each other's religious observances like Christmas and Chanukah. Recently they received a half-million dollar grant from the Luce Foundation to improve

Jewish/Christian cooperation even more.

Plus Andover Newton reaches out to Muslims. In 2009 they hosted the first-ever national dialog for Muslims and Baptists, two groups you don't often think of together. Another Muslim/Baptist Summit was hosted by the school in 2012. In a world where Jews, Christians, and Muslims too often are at odds, a school of our denomination is working hard to bring them together. It's what someone has labeled an "Abrahamic Family Reunion."

Second Timothy says: "All scripture is inspired by God and is useful for teaching, for reproof, for correction, and for training in righteousness..." (3:16). Sometimes a passage's usefulness lies in the negative example it sets. The book of Obadiah, depicting Edom's ugly betrayal of its "brother," Judea, and the prophet's bitter reaction, reminds me of fighting families and fighting families of religions.

The bad news is, families fight — and family fights hurt. The good news is, with the help of God, family fights can be resolved. For "nothing will be impossible with God."

Questions for Discussion

1. Review the story of the brothers Jacob and Esau. Whom does the biblical writer favor and why?

2. Does Jacob do anything to win God's favor? Is he deserving in some way? Isn't he the predatory one?

3. In this chapter we are given four steps to reconciliation of a family fight:
a. Be humble
b. Stay connected
c. Enlist help
d. Take the first step.
Are there bad feelings between members of your family? Hurt feelings? What are the obstacles preventing reconciliation? What could you do to resolve it?

4. Consider the idea of three religions as "family members." Is the comparison apt? Why or why not?

5. Do Christians have a calling to be peacemakers? What does that mean to you?

— Overview —
HABAKKUK

This prophet lived in Judea under King Jehoiakim (609-597 BCE), its next-to-the-last ruler. The Babylonian empire, also known as the Chaldeans, a "fierce and impetuous nation," was on the rise and threatening.

The book of Habakkuk unfolds in three sections. Verses 1:1—2:5 are a dialog between the prophet and the almighty. Habakkuk initially complains about injustice in his homeland: "(T)he law becomes slack and justice never prevails. The wicked surround the righteous — therefore judgment comes forth perverted" (1:4). God's answer to the prophet's complaint is unexpected. God is raising up the Chaldeans to punish the wicked of Judah (1:5-11)! Habakkuk finds using the even more wicked Babylonians to chastise the unrighteous of his nation quite unacceptable — and tells God (1:12-17). God responds that a day of judgment on Babylon also lies ahead (2:12-17).

This remarkable exchange is theologically significant. First, it asserts God is the God of all people and not just a tribal or national God. Judeans and Babylonians, everyone, near and far, ultimately will be held accountable for their actions. Second, this exchange also indicates almighty God is approachable. God graciously entertains the prophet's questions and complaints. So God's transcendence and immanence both are upheld.

Verses 2:6-20 list the woes that will befall wicked individuals and nations. It's reminiscent of Matthew 23:13-36. The adage, "What goes around, comes around" is asserted in 2:8a: "Because you (Babylon) have plundered many nations, all that survive will plunder you." This passage contains striking images such as "the very stones will cry out from the wall, and the plaster will respond from the woodwork," in the face of injustice (2:11).

Habakkuk closes with what various commentators have labeled a psalm or a poem. Verse 3:19c indicates it was to be set to music, specifically stringed instruments. In 3:2 Habakkuk prays, in effect: "Thy will be done, on earth as it is in heaven." Verses 3:3-16 are a powerful and beautifully written theophany, in which the prophet sees a vision of God ruling over earth and heaven and responds with fear and trembling. Again, this is high theology:

> *You split the earth with rivers. The mountains saw you, and writhed; a torrent of water swept by; the deep gave forth its voice. The sun raised high its hands; the moon stood still in its exalted place... In fury you trod the earth, in anger you trampled nations.*
> (Habakkuk 3:9b-12)

This short book is well worth reading! Any hymns, which lift up the power and majesty of God, could be good choices. Reginald Huber's majestic "Holy, Holy, Holy! Lord God Almighty" and

Isaac Watts' venerable "I Sing the Mighty Power of God" come to mind.

Children are familiar with not getting everything they ask for from their parent(s). They may also have experienced the frustration of unanswered prayer. For example, they prayed for a special toy at Christmas, but didn't get it. Or more seriously, prayed for the recovery of a pet or a relative, who died.

Recognition could be made that unanswered prayer may be upsetting. But an affirmation can be added that we can trust God. Loving parents long to provide what their child asks for, and will, when they can. Matthew 7:9-10 can be referenced with a piece of bread, a stone, a can of tuna fish, and a toy snake used to illustrate Jesus' parable. The point is, we trust parent(s) to do the right thing for their child(ren) — but also must trust their judgment. So also we must trust in the goodness and wisdom of God.

How to Get Your Prayers Answered
Habakkuk 3:2, 17-19

Prayer is one of the most frequently mentioned topics in the Bible. More than 500 passages mention praying. We are encouraged, again and again, to bring God our requests and concerns. We are assured, over and over, that God hears and answers prayers. Scripture is filled with reassuring words.

For example, "Whatever you ask in prayer with faith, you will receive," that's Jesus (Matthew 21:22). Or "Ask, and it will be given you; seek, and you will find; knock, and it will be opened to you," Jesus again (Luke 11:9 RSV). Saint Paul, in 1 Thessalonians, encourages us to "(P)ray without ceasing" (5:17). James reassures believers that "The prayer of the righteous is powerful and effective" (5:16b). All these verses are extremely positive. They seem to assume an immediate, deeply satisfying answer to our prayers.

But does that match your experience? Probably not always. I suspect most of us have sometimes felt like Habakkuk in the scripture lesson. This prophet wailed and railed against God, who seemed not to be paying attention. Habakkuk got angry with God. He shouted, "O Lord, how long shall I cry for help, and you will not listen? Or cry to you 'Violence!' and you will not save?" (1:2).

He planted himself on the city wall and challenged God to answer, "I will stand at my watch post, and station myself on the rampart; I will keep watch to see what (God) will say to me, and what (God) will answer concerning my complaint" (1:2; 2:1).

Habakkuk joins other Bible figures who prayed and prayed but felt unanswered: like barren Hannah, who, for years, asked for a child. She prayed so hard in the sanctuary at Shiloh that old Eli, the priest, thought she was drunk (1 Samuel 1:1-18). Or King David, who felt overwhelmed by enemies, and murmured: "How long, O Lord, will you look on (passively)? Rescue me from their ravages" (Psalm 35:17). Or Job, who felt abandoned by God. He complains: "I cry to you and you do not answer...! Stand, and you merely look at me" (30:20). Or Saint Paul, who prayed three times that his "thorn in the flesh" be lifted. But it wasn't (2 Corinthians 12:7b-9a).

All these folks struggled and you and I do, sometimes, with unanswered prayer. Which brings me to the subject of my sermon: How to get your prayers answered.

The good news is that prayer *always* is answered. That's right! Your prayers, and mine, always are answered. We just don't always get the answer we want or expect. When you think about it, that's often a blessing.

Country artist Garth Brooks, a self-professed Christian, has a song titled "Unanswered Prayers." It's on his album, *The Hits* (Capitol Records, 1994). This song is about the experience of meeting an old flame at a high school football game, years later. In that instant, the singer remembers how, as a teenager, he prayed *so hard* that this particular girl would always be his. He promised that, if God just granted his fervent prayer, he'd never bother God with anything else.

But things didn't work out between them. He and his girlfriend split. In time they each married somebody else. In the song, years later, standing next to his wife at the football game when he spies his old girlfriend, the singer gets what a blessing it was — what a gift of God it was — that his prayer wasn't answered. He sees that he and this girl were incompatible, and that his wife is so much better for him. Garth Brooks' song reminds me of a quote by Saint Teresa of Avila, "There are more tears shed over answered prayers than over unanswered prayers." Or of the bumper sticker I once saw: "Happiness isn't getting what you want. It's wanting what you've got."

Let's try a thought experiment. Imagine someone somewhere prayed to get a ticket on that first, famous voyage of the *Titanic*. It was, after all, the grandest, finest, fastest, and (allegedly) safest ship afloat. The passenger list read like "Who's Who." There were Astors and a Guggenheim, the owners of Macy's; Broadway producers, a countess, and an aide to the president; also prominent athletes, and, of course, Leonardo DiCaprio and Kate Winslet! What an opportunity to rub elbows for a week with the rich and famous! Isn't it possible someone prayed hard for a berth on the *Titanic*, but didn't get it?

Imagine his disappointment when the ship sailed without him. Maybe he was bitter when God said "No." "No" is an answer, after all; just not the answer he desired. Still, sometimes God doesn't answer our prayers the way we want because, as that old TV show put it, "Father Knows Best." Some of God's greatest gifts are unanswered prayers.

Other times God's answer to our prayer is "be patient and wait." Often it takes time for our prayers to ripen, like fruit on a vine. We may not yet be mature enough to receive the blessing we want. After all, maturity matters.

Parents don't give immature children everything they ask for no matter how much they whine. No parent in his or her right mind would give a nine-year-old a car to drive on the turnpike. They would not give their seven-year-old a loaded gun to play cowboys and Indians with his friends.

Good parents, concerned parents, loving parents make judgments based on the maturity of their children daily. God, our loving, heavenly parent makes that same kind of assessment of us. So sometimes God, in God's infinite wisdom and love, says: "You'll have to wait a while for a 'Yes' to that prayer. The answer is coming. Trust me!" (Ever hear that from parents?) You'll get that blessing in time. You just aren't ready yet. Sometimes the timing of a gift is really important.

Sometimes our sin blocks our prayers. Before we can pray effectively, we need to clean house. That's a blessing too. As we pray and wait and wait and pray, we slowly get our souls and ourselves back in order.

When a house spouse cleans house, she or he, throws out the rubbish. Hate, prejudice, bitterness, and resentment — all our sins — stand between a holy God and us. Our sins grieve God. Before we can come to God, we've got to clean up. As a saying attributed to Augustine puts it, we must "pray as if everything depended on God, but work as if everything depends on us."

Sometimes when praying we notice dirt in the corners of our hearts and minds that needs removing. If God says "No" to our prayers or makes us wait it's always for our good. As Jesus put it, if human fathers and mothers know how — and want to — give good gifts to their children, how much more does God yearn to give good gifts, the best, to you and me (see Matthew 7:7-11)? But only at the right time. That's part of the gift.

So we circle back to our starting issue: How to get your prayers answered. This topic is subtler than it seems. Every prayer is answered. Sometimes we just don't get the answer we expect and often that's a blessing.

Other times God's answer is "be patient and wait." We're not mature enough or ready to receive the blessing we seek. God, in God's great mercy, puts us off, like loving parents sometimes say "Not yet" to their child.

There's more. The last chapter of Habakkuk provides the perfect prayer. It's the one prayer that always is answered. It's part of the prayer Jesus taught. It's what he prayed himself in the Garden of Gethsemane. The perfect prayer that's always answered is "Thy will be done."

Jesus shaped his entire life to accord with God's will. Habakkuk, after complaining about unanswered prayer, eventually did the same. He came around in chapter 3: "O Lord, I have heard of your renown... I stand in awe... of your work."

The prophet continued, "In your own time revive (your will); in our own time make (your will) known." He concluded,

> *Though the fig tree does not blossom, and no fruit is on the vines; though the produce of the olive fails, and the fields yield no food; though the flock is cut off from the fold, and there is no herd in the stalls, yet I will rejoice in the Lord; I will exalt in the God of my salvation.*
> (Habakkuk 3:17-18)

Habakkuk said, in effect, "Thy will be done." He promised that even if things got bad, the crops dried up, the herds destroyed, he still would trust God. For, as the prophet put it: "God, the Lord is my strength; he makes my feet like the feet of a deer," an animal that treads safely in high and dangerous places (3:19).

The late James Montgomery Boice, longtime preacher on The Bible Study Hour commented on this passage. He noted a change in the prophet's tone. Boice wrote, "Earlier Habakkuk... prayed for God to change (God's) mind... However (the prophet) has gotten his mind off his own work now and desires the establishment of God's work... instead."

This, to Boice, is "the... final secret of effective prayer... petitions that are in accord with God's desires... Habakkuk prays that God's deeds, not his own deeds or desires, might be renewed."[1]

This passage reminds me that the best prayers are like an anchor. When you're in a boat and the anchor is out, and you're floating along or fishing, if you tug on the anchor rope, you don't pull the anchor to you. You pull the boat to the anchor.

Eventually the boat lines up with the anchor. The best prayers don't try to drag God to us. We can't. The best prayers draw us closer to God. The best prayers line us up with God's will. That's where this prophet eventually got to in his prayers. He started complaining. But as he prayed, his attitude changed.

Maybe Habakkuk came to realize prayer always is answered. Or that God's "No" can be for the best. Or that God's, "Wait a while, you're not ready yet" also is an answer. Or that there are corners of our soul that need cleaning before God can say "Yes."

For whatever reason Habakkuk offered the perfect prayer, the one which always is answered. It's the prayer Jesus taught us, the one he prayed in the Garden of Gethsemane, on the last night of his earthly life, as he faced the prospect of a terrible death.

How to get your prayers answered? Pray and mean it, "Not my will, but thy will be done. Thy will be done, on earth as it is in heaven." Then you, like Habakkuk, can "rejoice in the Lord" and "exalt in the God of (your) salvation" (3:18). For God hears and answers prayer according to what is best. That's the good news!

---

1. James Montgomery Boice, *The Minor Prophets, Volume 2: An Expository Commentary* (Grand Rapids: Baker Books, 1986), pp. 422-423.

Questions for Discussion

1. If God is going to do what he wants anyway, why pray?

2. When have your prayers been answered? Why do you think you received a favorable response?

3. What is the role of patience in this process?

4. Does God favor some people's prayers more than others? How can we be certain whether we are worthy of having our prayers answered?

5. What is the lesson Habakkuk had to learn? What is the perfect prayer that is always answered?

— Overview —
MALACHI

In the Christian Bible, Malachi is the last book before the New Testament. By contrast, the Jewish Scriptures — called the Old Testament by many Christians — end with 2 Chronicles. The number of books is the same: 39. But differences in their order are driven by theology. The Hebrew version of scripture ends on a triumphant note. King Cyrus of Persia is commanded by God to release the Babylonian captives and rebuild the temple in Jerusalem (2 Chronicles 36:22-23). The Christian version of the Old Testament ends somberly. Malachi describes at length the failures of the temple system and the corruption of its priesthood (Malachi 1:6—2:12). He closes by predicting Elijah's return and the coming of "the great and terrible day of the Lord" (Malachi 4:1-6). This is a prelude to the gospel identification of John the Baptist with Elijah, the epistle to the Hebrew's depiction of Jesus as our great high priest (chs. 5-8), and the Christian emphasis on Christ's second coming. Also, Malachi sounds a universalistic note. Verse 1:11 depicts all nations worshiping God. This is a precursor to the early church's outreach ministry to the Gentiles.

The book of Malachi is structured in a question-and-answer format, rather like a court case.

God is the Prosecutor and Israel the Defendant. The charges include not recognizing God's providence in choosing Israel/Jacob over its neighboring "brother" nation of Edom/Esau (1:2-5; see also Obadiah 10-15); priestly misconduct (1:6—2:9); not honoring marriage (2:13-17); injustice against the weakest members of society, including hired workers, widows, orphans, and the stranger (3:5); and not paying the tithe (3:8-12).

Malachi's style is vivid, providing memorable images. These images include characterizing Elijah's coming judgment as "a refiner's fire," which purifies gold and silver, or as a "fuller's soap," which bleaches clothing (3:2b-4). Or presenting the coming day of the Lord as an "oven" that will burn up the arrogant evildoers like "stubble" (4:1). Malachi concludes with lovely images: "(F)or you who revere my name the sun of righteousness shall rise, with healing in its wings. You shall go out leaping like calves from the stall" (4:2). Charles Wesley quotes the first part of this verse in his beloved Christmas carol, "Hark! The Herald Angels Sing."

Malachi was written around 460 BCE, when Israel was a subject nation of the Persian empire, ruled by a governor (1:8). The temple had been rebuilt, but was only a shadow of its former glory. The population suffered from crop failures and locusts (3:10b-11), and worship was characterized by laxity and indifference. The prophet offers hope. But first God's people must reform, in part by taking sacrifice seriously. Hymns related to these themes include Brian Doerksen's contemporary praise song "Refiner's Fire," based on Malachi 3:2a-3 and

Francis Havergal's classic "Take My Life and Let It Be," particularly the stewardship verse missing from many modern hymnals:

> *Take my lips and let them be*
> *Filled with messages from Thee;*
> *Take my silver and my gold*
> *Not a mite would I withhold.*

A children's message can be built around offerings. Many church schools include an offering during Sunday school to accustom youngsters to giving. No doubt they also have observed the ushers taking the collection during worship.

The parable of the widow's mite (Mark 12:41-44) teaches this and could be retold, contrasting a wad of dollar bills — not costly to the wealthy giver — with two pennies, which represented everything the widow had.

What Jesus noted was not the amount, but the love and self-sacrifice with which her gift was given. Children may not have finances to share. But they can give of themselves in acts of lovingkindness and devotion. What's important is not what we give, but that we strive to give our best. Being reminded of this is affirming for them.

Don't Rob God!
Malachi 3:8-12

An upsetting event took place in a country village. The one local church was robbed.

This small congregation in a village of 250 never locked the church doors. Anyone was free to come in and pray any time of the day or night. Some did, even after midnight. The restrooms always were available for passersby to use. Many residents in the village kept their own home doors unlocked too. They just trusted each other.

Then one Saturday the janitors discovered the church had been robbed the night before. The entire sound system, worth multiple thousands of dollars, was stolen from its cabinet. Small items like cassette players were taken from Sunday school. It looked like the thieves had inside knowledge. They knew what to look for and where to find it. For example, a microphone not easily seen was taken from under a piano.

The robbery sent a shock wave through the town. Church members felt violated and vulnerable. Since then, the church doors are locked and there is a little less trust in the town. After all, if someone would rob a church, what else might they do?

Stealing from a church is always shocking, isn't it? It makes you wonder, "Is nothing sacred anymore?" Even more upsetting is when a pastor steals from his or her parishioners. From time to time we read such stories in the news. As when a 74-year-old priest from Buffalo was caught stealing $214,000 from his parish. Or the Baptist leader a few years back who embezzled $600,000 from his denomination. (After prison, he ran for president of the same denomination! He lost.)

But stealing from God is nothing new. Malachi knew this 460 years before Christ. In chapter 1 of his book he accuses the temple priesthood of robbing God. They were to sacrifice unblemished lambs on the altar.

However, the priests were selling or keeping the good sheep and only sacrificing the weak ones: the lame, sick, or blind — animals that were worth less, or worthless. God found this insulting. The governor would not accept second-rate gifts (1:8). So, why offer leftovers to God?

Then the prophet turns his attention from the priests to the average worshiper. In the passage we read, Malachi, speaking for God, complains about the tithe. Or rather about people not paying the full tithe. Giving the tithe is commanded in Leviticus (27:30). The Israelites were to dedicate the first tenth of everything to God.

The way the tithe was calculated changed over the years. When the Hebrews were wandering in the desert, they had only sheep to give. So once yearly each flock was counted, and every tenth (healthy) lamb that passed under the shepherd's staff was brought to the altar and sacrificed, given to God. It's a good thing sheep can't count!

I should offer an aside here. The idea of animal sacrifice understandably is upsetting to our present-day sensibilities. Many laws rightly protect animals in twenty-first-century America. But in ancient cultures, animal sacrifice was widespread, maybe even universal. For Judaism, this practice ended with the destruction of the second Jerusalem Temple.

Later, as the Israelites settled in the Promised Land, they were established as farmers and also had crops to share. So 10% of the harvest was weighed out, at the ancient equivalent of a grain elevator, and turned over to the temple. The grain was used to feed the temple priests and their families, or given to refugees, widows, and orphans, or sold to pay the upkeep on temple buildings.

So tithing originated in Leviticus and went through changes to adjust to different circumstances. But no matter what form it took, tithing was an acknowledgment that a substantial portion of the Israelite's income was to be set aside for God. Tithing was a way of fulfilling the Great Commandment, to love the Lord with all your heart, soul, and mind, and love your neighbor as yourself (Matthew 22:26).

The tithe was understood as owed to God. Not to pay it, or to shortchange it, was theft. Malachi knew this. In pointed words he asks, "Will anyone rob God?" "Yet," God complains, "you are robbing me!" In the back-and-forth format used in this book, the people ask: "How are we robbing (God)?" God answers, "In your tithes and offerings... (Y)ou are robbing me — the whole nation of you!" Speaking through the prophet, God complains: "Bring the *full tithe* into the storehouse" (3:8-10a, emphasis added). To Malachi, both the temple priests switching animals and the common people shorting the tithe were stealing from God.

Malachi brings up tithing. Some may have questions about this practice. One could be, "What's the theology behind tithing?" Actually tithing means lots of things. It's an act of thanksgiving, charity, and worship. But especially for believers, it's an act of faith.

If you or I give 10% of our income to charity, instead of spending it on ourselves or our family, or investing it with a broker or banker, that's a faith statement. We're taking a leap of faith assuming God will provide and that we can and will get by on 90%.

Our mortgage payments may loom large, our job may not be secure, taxes continue, medical problems or retirement may be on the horizon, we could be saving for college, our kid may need braces, we might have to replace a car, heating costs and the price of gas are up. In the face of financial pressures, it's an act of faith to give up one tenth of our income to charity, trusting that God knows what we need and can and will provide. Tithing is a sign we believe God knows us and loves us like a caring parent and that we rely on God.

Also, as Malachi puts it, tithing is a way of putting God to the test. That's what God says in one of the verses we read, "(P)ut me to the test, says the Lord God of hosts; see if I will not open the windows of heaven for you and pour down for you overflowing blessing" (v. 10b). In other words, God doesn't mind being challenged or tested.

You might wonder, "Is tithing a requirement for getting into heaven? If we don't tithe, will we not be saved?" As near as I can tell, that answer is "No." (Big sigh of relief.) Christianity is a religion of grace, not law. The only thing required for salvation is we believe in the death and resurrection of Jesus Christ. We're not sub-Christian if we give 9 1/2% to charity and super-Christian if we 11%.

Another question: How does tithing work practically? There are at least two ways to tithe, the "straight tithe" and the "modern tithe." Some churches, usually fundamentalist, expect their members to give 10% of their gross income, without adjustment, to their church. You can't join unless you tithe. In some cases, you're expected to give to your church only, nothing else.

By contrast, at least some denominational literature from our United Church of Christ suggests giving the "modern tithe," 5% of our total income, to charity. The modern tithe acknowledges the burden of taxes, and that our taxes, which help fight poverty, support health care, and underwrite education, work for the common good. Taxes do some things the ancient temple charity system used to do. The modern tithe also recognizes non-church organizations, like the United Way, Red Cross, Scout groups, or Church World Service/CROP, also do God's work and deserve support.

Is the modern tithe valid? Or is it robbing God? In our denomination, the individual worshiper must decide. As I said earlier, it is true the practice of tithing has changed over the years.

But some will say even 5% is more than they can manage. It's "too hard." But isn't Jesus' command to love our enemies also hard? Aren't there always challenges in following Christ? Every part of being a Christian is demanding, not just finances.

Plus, survey after survey has found the overwhelming majority of people who tithe the full 10% are more than satisfied with the practice. They're glad to stretch themselves. Things work out okay for their families. Giving sacrificially and seeing the good it does makes them feel better. Saint Paul says "God loves a cheerful giver" (2 Corinthians 9:7). Millions of Christians cheerfully give 10% of their total income away.

As one tither put it, "Tithing has taught me to manage my money better. Giving 10% of my income to charity has made me more conscious and careful of how I spend the remaining 90%. I'm a better money manager because I tithe."

Tithing has a long history behind it. It's sound theologically. It's a thank you to God. It shows we walk the walk, not just talk the talk. It's a way of loving our neighbor as ourselves. Jesus said, "No one can serve two masters. Either he will hate the one and love the other, or he will be devoted to the one and despise the other. (We) cannot serve both God and money."

He said, "I tell you, do not worry about your life, what you will eat or drink; or about your body, what you will wear. Is not life more important than food, and the body more important than (clothing)?"

He reminded us, "Look at the birds of the air (like the birds landing in our backyards in the fall) they do not sow or reap or store away in barns, and yet your heavenly Father feeds them. Are you not much more valuable than they? Who of you by worrying can add a single hour to (their) life?" (In fact, worrying takes away from the length of your life.)

He asked, "Why do you worry about clothes? See how the lilies of the field grow. They do not labor or spin. Yet I tell you that not even Solomon in all his splendor was (arrayed) like one of these. If... God (so) clothes the grass of the field, which is here today and tomorrow is thrown into the fire, will he not much more clothe (us)...?"

He said, "So do not worry, saying, 'What shall we eat?' or 'What shall we drink?' or 'What shall we wear?' For the (Gentiles seek) all these things, and (God) knows that (we) need them. But seek first (God's) kingdom and... righteousness, and all these things will be given to you as well" (Matthew 6:24-33 NIV, adapted).

Bill Hybels, well-known pastor of Willow Creek Church, said tithing forces us to take "a heart check, a gut check, and a faith check." Heart check: do we love God more than money? Gut check: do we trust God? Faith check: do we believe God's promises?

Another preacher asks us to consider tithing from God's perspective. He offers an illustration that runs something like this. Imagine you've built your own business. For decades you've poured your blood, sweat, and tears into making it successful. Finally, after much struggle, it's going great. Your adult children beg to be let in and help you run it. You agree and set it up. They all get equal shares.

You trust your children to do what's right. All you ask is that they run your business well. But instead of, say, investing 10%, they rob the business blind. They take everything you've worked and suffered for, with no respect for your feelings and spend it on themselves.

The business fails. Which hurts more, losing the company? Or betrayal by those you trusted? I'd guess your family's unwillingness to do the right thing and respect you hurts more. Maybe that's a bit like how God feels when we take what God deserves and spend it on ourselves.

You probably now know much more than you ever wanted to know about Malachi and tithing! So let me end this sermon with a question. Is the tithe, a full 10%, or the modern tithe, 5%, a goal we will accept or at least strive toward? Will we pledge to increase our giving by one or two or three percent more of our income, so we're heading in the right direction?

Tithing, or stretching toward it, is an important step for us in learning to trust and obey — and in loving God and neighbor. God, after all, cared enough to send the very best, his only beloved Son. Will we care enough to give God what's due? As Malachi put it, "Will anyone rob God?" (3:8).

Questions for Discussion

1. Review God's complaint against Israel. Which are our society's faults as well?

2. How can we teach responsible giving to our children?

3. Why did God complain about not getting the full measure of the tithe? After all, he can't really use it.

4. Compare and contrast the "straight tithe" and the "modern tithe."

5. How does the practice of tithing improve our relationship with God? How could it make us better people?

— Overview —
HAGGAI

Many of the Minor Prophets are difficult to date. This is not the case with Haggai. His chronology was extremely precise. Verse 1:1 states the word of the Lord came to Haggai on "the second year of King Darius, in the sixth month, on the first day of the month." In the Christian calendar, that's August 29, 520 BCE. The fifteenth verse of that same chapter depicts the people returning to work on the temple 24 days later, or September 17. According to verse 2:1, Haggai received and passed on another prophecy on the twenty-first day of the seventh month, or October 17. Verses 2:10 and 2:20-23 are from December 18 of the same year. So this book documents a ministry taking place within just three months and three weeks.

Almost nothing is known about Haggai himself. His name can be translated "Festival," and may be a diminutive of "born on a feast day" or "festival of the Lord." Haggai additionally diminished his own importance. Nowhere does the prophet speak in his own voice. Rather the Lord speaks through Haggai twenty or more times in this brief book. He makes frequent use of repetition. Five times the people are encouraged to "consider" their situation. Three times in one verse, Zerubbabel the governor, Joshua, the high priest and the common people are told to "take courage" (2:4).

This was fitting. In Haggai's time there was much to overcome. Judea no longer was free, but rather a weakened vassal of the larger Persian empire under Darius. Economic conditions were hard. Verses 1:5-6, 10-11 depict famine, inflation, and drought. Verse 2:17 speaks of crop-destroying blight, mildew, and hail. Plus the restoration of the temple, begun some twenty years earlier, had ground to a halt, due to opposition from the surrounding peoples and a lack of commitment by God's people. Courage indeed was needed.

Earlier prophets, including Isaiah, Jeremiah, and Malachi, had been critical of empty formalism in worship or priestly abuses in the temple, but not Haggai. The Lord, speaking through this prophet, insisted the temple must be rebuilt. This is not because God needed the people's worship. Or because they could earn God's favor through works of righteousness. Rather their national life had to be centered again on worshiping God. That's a message that's always fitting.

Hymns related to Haggai include several classics. James Russell Lowell's "Once to Every Man and Nation" provides a call to action. "Built on the Rock"; "I Love Thy Kingdom, Lord"; and "We Would Be Building" celebrate the church.

Children may have some difficulty envisioning "the old days." Seek "Remember When" nostalgia booklets that can make the past come alive. There's one for every year, back to the early twentieth century. Time lines cover major events from each year. Photos show advertisements, hair and clothing styles, and cars.

It might be fun to find and share the pastor's birth year and have the children note how much things have changed. After this introductory exercise, the point could be made that change is inevitable. "To everything there is a season," as Ecclesiastes puts it (3:1). Still, the one thing that never changes is God's love for us. "Remember When" booklets can be found in many greeting card shops. Or Seek Publishing can be contacted at 1055 Ridgecrest Drive, Millersville, Tennessee 37072 (SeekPublishing.com).

These ARE the Good Old Days!
Haggai 2:1-5

Most of us, I think, can relate to this experience: sitting around with a group of friends or relatives and playing "Remember when?" Remember when a hamburger cost fifteen cents? I do, which dates me. Remember when the Mustang came out? Or the '55 T-Bird? Or the Edsel? Remember when you could buy a house you could live in for $20,000?

Games of "Remember when" seem nostalgic, don't they? The past, once it's behind us, seems bathed in a golden light. Those were the days when men were men, finances were fine, households were happier, neighbors were nicer, children were politer, and sermons seemed shorter! As Archie and Edith Bunker sang, at the start of "All in the Family":

> Boy the way Glen Miller played. Songs that made the hit parade,
> Guys like us we had it made, those were the days.
> And you know where you were then, girls were girls and men were men,
> Mister we could use a man like Herbert Hoover again.
> Didn't need no welfare states everybody pulled his weight,

> Gee our old LaSalle ran great, those were the days![1]

Quoting this dates me again!

An echo of Archie Bunker-esque "remember when" is heard in Haggai. Given the conditions, this was understandable. It was 520 BCE. The Judeans had been in exile for almost fifty years. Their nation lost its independence. The Jerusalem Temple was destroyed and their city with it.

When a remnant straggled back, half a century later, they were a second-rate vassal of the vast Persian empire. They started to rebuild the temple, but the surrounding peoples opposed them. The project ground to a halt (see Ezra 1-4).

Their nation was beset by poverty and famine. Haggai describes their situation: "You have sown much, and harvested little; you eat, but never enough; you drink, but you never have your fill; you cloth yourselves, but no one is warm; and you that earn wages put them into a bag with holes" (Haggai 1:6). Actually, that last part, "You that earn wages put them into a bag with holes" sounds familiar, doesn't it? Ever feel like your paycheck goes into a bag with holes?

In those discouraging days I imagine some of the oldsters played "remembered when." They looked back some seventy years, when the temple stood in its former glory. The gap between how they remembered it, and how they lived then left them discouraged. "Remember when?" can be fun, or it can make you depressed.

Remember when Mainline Protestant churches, every single Sunday, were filled with people? Some do. A pastor found a big, panoramic picture of his church taken sixty years earlier. He shared it with his congregation one Sunday morning. The photo was taken on Palm Sunday. The Confirmation Class, in white, was sitting proudly up front. In this wonderful old photo, every seat was filled. A few men were standing. Every adult male was neatly dressed in a suit and tie. Every adult woman was wearing a hat. The entire congregation of 350 looked up dutifully at the preacher. Every child appears well behaved. No one was asleep.

The present-day pastor commented, "We could look at this photo and say, 'Remember when? Remember the glory days of Mainline American churches? Remember when sanctuaries were full, worshipers were attentive, and children sat quietly? Those were the good old days. If we only could go back!'"

He was right. Things aren't the same. We're living in what has been labeled "The postChristian Era." Church no longer occupies a central place in our society. When I was a kid, growing up in New England, there were "blue laws." Stores couldn't open on Sunday until after worship. Today you can shop 24/7!

When I was a kid, athletic events were never on Sunday mornings. Today youth soccer and basketball tournaments typically happen Sunday all day. Recently a marathon was held on Sunday morning. There were 15,000 runners and 300,000-400,000 spectators around the race route all morning. That's a third of a million people not in worship — and I don't think all of them were Muslims or Jews.

When I was a kid, my mother never worked outside the home. Not that she didn't have plenty to do — three children and a husband who often worked fifty hours a week. Still she had time and energy for volunteering, mostly at church. Mom was a Sunday school teacher, and in Knit-Wits, a sewing group that created lap robes for shut-ins. She visited nursing homes and the sick on behalf of the church and went to weekday Bible studies. In our congregation, in the 1950s, there were dozens of housewives like her: a wellspring of willing workers.

Today 75% of American women work outside the home. And 75% of those who work outside the home are employed full-time. When they come home, after working all day, most pull what sociologist Arlie Hochschild called "The Second Shift." They go to work again, cleaning, cooking, and paying bills. Consequently, by Sunday morning, Mom and Dad are exhausted. They sleep in. Things aren't what they used to be, for families or churches.

We may long for "the good old days." But, other than Daylight Savings Time, once a year in the fall, no one can turn back the clock. The "glory days" of the mainline church may not come again, just like the second temple, started around Haggai's time, wasn't the same as Solomon's Temple, finished 400 years earlier.

Still, the word of the Lord comes to us, a faithful remnant, just as it came to believers in Haggai's time: "Yet now take courage... says the Lord... take courage, all you people... work, for I am with you... My spirit abides among you; do not fear" (Haggai 2:4-5). My spirit abides in you; do not fear. Don't get discouraged! For one thing, the good old days may not have been as good as they seem. Was there ever a Golden Age for the church?

The book of Acts depicts the first Christians living in harmony. "All who believed were together and had all things in common; they would sell their possessions and goods and distribute the proceeds to all, as any had need," Acts says. It continues, "Day by day, as they spent much time together in the temple, they broke bread at home, and ate their food with glad and generous hearts, praising God and having the goodwill of all the people..." (2:43-47a).

Sounds idyllic, doesn't it? Until you read the letters of Paul. Consider the church at Corinth. Church members were fighting over preachers. (It happened even then!) Some favored Paul, others Peter, some Apollos. Others claimed the "high road" and said they belonged to Christ (1 Corinthians 1:10-13).

Some in the congregation were involved in sexual scandals (1 Corinthians 5—6:12-20). Others were suing one another (1 Corinthians 6:1-11). Worshipers pushed and shoved during communion (1 Corinthians 11:17-34). There was no perfection in the church at Corinth!

Nor were the 1950s flawless. The pastor I mentioned earlier pointed out some other things in the old church photo. There were more than 350 people in church. But only five were smiling. He encouraged churchgoers to check it out themselves. He wondered, "Where's the excitement? Where's the joy? Were these God's chosen people?"

Commentators remember the stifling conformity of the 50s, the age of the "organization man" in the gray flannel suit. It was difficult to be different. I recall a lack of concern for civil rights, the environment, social justice, or women's rights. Maybe the 1950s weren't the "Greatest Generation" either. Maybe, as songwriter Billy Joel put it, we should "Say goodbye to the oldies, but goodies, because the good old days weren't always good and tomorrow ain't as bad as it seems."

One songwriter put it more elegantly in 1844. It also was a challenging time for churches. Our nation, and many congregations, were divided over slavery. One American in seven wasn't free. James Russell Lowell was an Abolitionist and social prophet. He called Christians to stand up for justice in a powerful hymn. Lowell wrote:

> *Once to every man and nation Comes the moment to decide,*
> *In the strife of truth with falsehood, For the good or evil side;*
> *New occasions teach new duties, Time makes ancient good uncouth;*
> *They must upward still and onward, Who would keep abreast of truth.*
> ("Once to Every Man and Nation")

The author of Ecclesiastes put it differently: "To everything there is a season, and a time for every purpose under heaven" (3:1 KJV). This happens to be Reformation Sunday. That the church should be constantly in reform is the great Protestant principle. Rather than yearning for the past, which we can't regain anyway, we are called to live into God's future. That means being faithful in present challenges.

Our church is different from what it was in the 50s. Our society is different too. What does it mean to be the church here and now in a post-Christian era? It means we can't wait passively for worshipers to flock to our doors like they did sixty years ago. They don't come and won't come. We have to go out to them. That means we have to change.

Let me tell you what one congregation is doing to adapt to the times. One summer a group of church members thought hard about ways their church could reach out to its community. They met in someone's kitchen. So they called themselves the Kitchen Cabinet. One conclusion they came to and passed to their leadership is their congregation needs to capitalize more on its strengths.

One thing that church does better than most is the arts. It has a superior music program. Its chancel choir and bell choir number more than forty. They have a children's choir, a 'tween-age choir, youth chimers, and a women's ensemble. Every worship service a "Sister Act," two actual sisters who are gifted musicians, play duets, most of which they arrange themselves on piano and organ.

Over the years this church has sponsored concerts, like a Messiah Sing, featuring soloists from a nearby symphony chorus. They've hosted a nationally known bell choir. It's a congregation blessed with numerous artists and some significant works by local artists hang on church walls. Religion and art have a long and strong connection. So the Kitchen Cabinet suggested their congregation make a more conscious effort to reach new people through the arts.

What might that look like? Perhaps an "arts corner" could be established, where paintings by local artists rotate monthly. Or a built-in cabinet created, where 3D arts, like pottery, could be displayed. This church's community has a small Arts Center, which offers a summer arts camp that has grown too big for their building. They have to turn children away. The newly arts-focused congregation offered to host the program in their large Fellowship Hall.

Their building was filled with kids for two weeks that summer, as they gathered for one week of arts and crafts and one week of drama. Each week culminated with children's art show or a play. Some of the children — and their parents — developed a new connection with the church that cared enough to reach out to them.

In future years, might that congregation celebrate their stained glass, the best in their city and use it as a springboard for stained-glass workshops for adults? For that congregation, could the arts be a vehicle for meeting new people and drawing them in to worship? Other churches in other settings will need to try different approaches. But all congregations have strengths. Can they capitalize on their strengths?

In every time and place God's people are challenged. That's where an occasional backward glance helps. We can't repeat the 1950's approach in the first decade of a new century. Insanity is doing the same old things over and over again, but expecting different results, as Einstein said. Or as James Russell Lowell put it, "New occasions teach new duties; time makes ancient good uncouth." You can never go back.

But we can remind ourselves that congregations overcame challenges in the past. Consider one church. There was the challenge of starting a new church from scratch in 1850; the challenge of coping with a painful split just a few decades later, as two groups left to found their own churches.

The church's ancestors weathered that crisis and built a new and bigger sanctuary within ten years. They added on in 1901, and again in the 1960s, to cope with new growth. None of those changes were easy. All of them were costly. But the church moved forward and adapted as required.

Churches have proven strong in the past. They can be strong again. Every congregation can look back, remember the past, and meditate on their church's greatness. That's like the people in Haggai's day remembering the grandeur of Solomon's Temple.

But, let's not get stuck in the past. Instead, let's recall the encouraging word of the Lord, as delivered through the prophet:

> *(T)ake courage... says the Lord... take courage, all you people... work, for I am with you... My spirit abides among you; do not fear...*
> (Haggai 2:4-5)

Followed by the promise:

> *The latter splendor of this house shall be greater than the former, says the Lord of hosts; and in this place I will give prosperity, says the Lord.*
> (Haggai 2:9)

Let's live as Christ's church today in such a way that we can look back and say, "The early 2000s: these ARE the good old days."

---

1. Quoted by permission of Alfred Music Publishing Company, Inc.

Questions for Discussion

1. The Overview to this sermon states: "Rather their national life had to be centered again on worshiping God." Find parallels between Haggai's time and our own. Can you envision a return in the United States to a life "centered again on worshiping God"? How might such a thing come to pass?

2. Find three wonderful things from the past that you would have liked to keep. Then find three things from today that are also worthy of keeping.

3. Project into the future, say twenty to thirty years from now. Will it be more or less God-centered? What must we do to make a more God-centered future?

4. What simple things might we do to "buck the trend"?

5. What strengths does your congregation have that could be used to attract the outside community? First inventory what currently is done. Then critique and expand.

— Overview —
ZECHARIAH

The prophets Haggai and Zechariah both were from Judea and were roughly contemporaries. The former's writings can be dated precisely on the Christian calendar. According to Haggai 1:1 and 2:1, his ministry took place between August 29 and October 17 of 520 BCE. The book of Zechariah also provides dates. According to verse 1:1, "the word of the Lord" came to this prophet in the eighth month of the second year of Darius of Persia, or October-November 520 BCE. Verse 1:7 states he received his first vision a few months later, on February 15, 519 BCE. In 7:1 we are told the word of the Lord again came to the prophet on December 7, 518 BCE. Nehemiah 12:16 lists Zechariah as a priest, but his book makes no mention of the dedication of the restored temple in the spring of 515 BCE. As a priest, it's likely Zechariah would have noted an event of this significance. So it's reasonable his ministry began in the latter half of 520 BCE but probably ended before 515 BCE.

Zechariah is named the son of Berechiah and grandson of Iddo in verse 1:1. Nothing more is known about the prophet's family. His name means "the Lord has remembered." In addition to his priestly role, Zechariah was the recipient of ecstatic visions. Chapters 1-6 describe eight visions in detail. This is apocalyptic literature, similar to the book of Revelation. In fact, there are numerous parallels between the books. For example, Zechariah's first vision, in 1:7-17, is of four horsemen. This is echoed in the famous Four Horsemen of the Apocalypse in Revelation chapter 6. Zechariah's fifth vision includes seven golden lampstands. So does Revelation 1:12. Some commentators note more than a dozen connections between these apocalyptic books, making it likely John of Patmos, the author of Revelation was familiar with Zechariah.

Chapters 1-8 are a unified whole and can be ascribed to the prophet himself. Chapters 9-14 are more problematic. Scholars sometimes label chapters 9-11 Zechariah II and 12-14 Zechariah III. The latter subsections are miscellaneous collections of oracles in no particular order. All three "books" of Zechariah begin with the phrase "The word of the Lord" (see 1:1; 9:1; 12:1). But that's about their only similarity. Zechariah II and III share little with Zechariah chapters 1-8 or with each other.

Hymns related to Zechariah include Georg Weissel's venerable "Lift Up Your Heads, O Mighty Gates" and the contemporary praise song, "The King of Glory Comes."

Holman Hunt's well-known painting of Christ as *The Light of the World* is a good beginning place for a children's lesson. Many churches have one, and many youngsters will have seen this depiction of Jesus. He's holding a lamp outside a closed door and knocking on it. Some of the details might be pointed out. The fact that there is no latch on the outside of the door is significant. Jesus never forces himself on anyone. Instead he waits quietly and patiently for us to hear his voice, see him there, and invite him into our lives. The only power Jesus relies on is his example of long-suffering love. Can the children imagine him there? Will they — and we — invite him into our hearts?

Behold, Your King Is Coming!
Zechariah 9:9-10

We're nearing the end of our yearlong series on "The Not-So-Minor Prophets." It has been a long journey. Our first featured prophet was Amos. He began his ministry about 760 years before Christ. Month by month we've been moving closer to the birth of Jesus and the Christian era.

As we've seen, some of the Minor Prophets are easy to interpret and others are more difficult. Jonah tells a story a child can understand. In fact, we often tell children the tale of Jonah and the whale. Obadiah is simple too. It has one theme: God will punish Edom.

Zechariah, by contrast, is complex. As our Overview notes, this book may be three collections cobbled together. Chapters 1-8 are dated precisely, ascribed to Zechariah, and portray eight successive visions. But the remainder of Zechariah is obscure. There are lots of different images in no apparent order. One Bible scholar calls these passages "disconnected."

Still, in spite of its obscurity — or maybe because of it — the Christian scriptures often allude to Zechariah. The gospel writers especially found predictions of the coming Messiah here. Among the 66 books in the Protestant Old Testament, Zechariah is second only to Isaiah in verses the early church connected with Jesus. One commentator found 22 references to Jesus as Messiah in Zechariah. Some you'll recognize right off.

For example, chapter 9:9 is a favorite Palm Sunday scripture:

> *Rejoice greatly, O daughter Zion! Shout aloud, O daughter Jerusalem! Lo, your king comes to you... humble and riding on a donkey, on a colt, the foal of a donkey.*

Chapter 11 mentions thirty pieces of silver (v. 12b), the price paid to Judas for betraying Jesus. That same chapter speaks, as does Jesus, about good and bad shepherds (see John 10).

Chapter 12:10 mentions one whose side is pierced, over whom Jerusalem weeps. The gospel of John understands this as a prophecy of the cross (see 19:37). Zechariah 13:7 says: "Strike the shepherd, that the sheep may be scattered." Jesus himself quoted this at the Last Supper (see Matthew 26:31; Mark 14:27).

Christians find Zechariah rich in references to Jesus, even though the original writer was not thinking of him. After all, Jesus' birth was 520 years in the future. Still, from our perspective, these words are prophetic. They tell believers our Savior and king is coming. But what kind of king would he be?

Surprising and paradoxical! Christianity has more paradoxes than any other major religion. G.K. Chesterton, that eccentric English wit, novelist, and defender of the faith wrote extensively on the paradoxes of Christianity (cf., ch. 5 of his book, *Orthodoxy*). Chesterton called paradox "truth standing on her head to gain (our) attention."

Consider some of the paradoxes of Christianity. We profess you have to die to live. Jesus said, "(T)hose who want to save their life will lose it, and those who lose their life for my sake will find it" (Matthew 16:25). We proclaim the meek and seemingly weak — not the powerful — will inherit the earth (Matthew 5:5). We affirm to be great you must be a servant (Matthew 20:26). We worship a king who is peaceful and humble, one who came not to lord it over us, but to self-sacrifice.

What a contrast between Jesus and other leaders. Too often men in power get drunk on prestige. Adolf Hitler adopted the title "The Fuhrer," which means "The Guide" of the Nazi nation. Thousands of goose-stepping, "Heil-Hitler" saluting storm troopers paraded for him. Manuel Noriega declared himself the "Maxim Leader" of Panama and ruled with an iron fist. Nicholae Ceausescu claimed to be "The Genius of the Carpathians." He had over thirty volumes of his speeches published. Even though his countrymen in Romania were among the poorest in Europe, Ceausescu owned 21 palaces, 40 villas, and 20 hunting retreats.

Ferdinand Marcos claimed to be "The Man of Destiny," beloved by his people. At the same time he put thousands of Philippine opponents in jail. His wife, Imelda, used a diamond-studded comb worth $44,000. Her closet held 2,000 pairs of shoes!

The Shah of Iran called himself "King of Kings," "Light of Lights," and "Occupier of the Peacock Throne." He spent a hundred million dollars on a party to celebrate the thirtieth anniversary of his reign. Next door, Saddam Hussein blanketed Iraq with murals and statues of himself and honored himself with parades featuring Soviet-made missiles.

Hitler, Noriega, Ceausescu, Marcos, The Shah, Saddam put their faith in ostentatious wealth and military might and cloaked themselves in grandiose titles. They were men who would be king. But the trash heap of history has claimed them all.

Hitler committed suicide in his bunker in Berlin as the Soviets closed in. Noriega languishes in a Miami prison. If he lives to complete his sentence, he'll be released at 92. Ceausescu was gunned down by a firing squad. Marcos died a lonely exile in Hawaii. The Shah of Iran died of cancer at age 60, a fugitive, with a price on his head.

Slobodan Milosevic, former Serbian strongman, died in prison, after a five-year trial. After a trial, Saddam Hussein's own people hanged him. These are only a few examples of dictators that failed. Meanwhile, the paradoxical king described in Zechariah marches on for 2,000 years.

Two millennia ago he rode into Jerusalem on the back of a donkey, a gentle beast of burden, a farm animal, a symbol of peace, just as the prophet predicted. He claimed no title for himself, except the Son of Man. He sought no crown, except a crown of thorns. The only way he was ever lifted up in his lifetime was on a cross.

But this year, and every year, two billion people will celebrate his birthday. This year and every year, the story of his life will be the most popular book sold. His last meal is remembered and celebrated somewhere in the world every hour. Hundreds of millions wear a cross, a reminder of him around their necks, close to the heart.

The one recorded prayer he taught his disciples is the best-known and most-repeated prayer in history. And sometimes, at the mere mention of his name, strong men and women weep. More thought has been devoted to this man's life, more books written about him, more good done in his name than any other person who ever lived. Just as the prophet Zechariah predicted, his dominion is from "sea to sea... to the ends of the earth" (9:10).

A noted Yale historian, Kenneth Latourette, put it like this:

> "No life ever lived on this planet has been so influential in the affairs of men as that of Christ. From that brief life, and its apparent frustration, has flowed a more powerful force for the triumphal waging of man's long battle than any other known in the human race."
>
> He continued, "Through it, millions of people have had their inner conflicts resolved. Through it, hundreds of millions have been lifted from illiteracy and ignorance and have been placed upon the road of growing intellectual freedom and control over the physical environment. It has done more to allay the physical ills of disease and famine than any other impulse, and it has emancipated millions from chattel slavery and millions of others from thralldom to vice. It has protected tens of millions from exploitation by their fellows, and it has been the most fruitful source of movements to lessen the horrors of war and to put the relations of men and nations on the basis of justice and peace."[1]

Another writer, Henry G. Bosch, said this:

> *Jesus painted no pictures; yet, some of the finest paintings of Raphael, Michelangelo, and Leonardo da Vinci received their inspiration from him. Jesus wrote no poetry; but he inspired Dante, Milton, and scores of the world's greatest poets. Jesus composed no music; still Haydn, Handel, Beethoven, Bach, and Mendelssohn reached their highest perfection of melody in the hymns, symphonies, and oratories they composed in His praise. Every sphere of human greatness has been enriched by this humble Carpenter of Nazareth.*[2]

Bosch noted Socrates taught for forty years, Plato for fifty, Aristotle for forty, and Jesus for only three. But the influence of his three-year ministry far outweighs the impact of the 130 years of teaching from men who were arguably the greatest thinkers who ever lived.

Twenty centuries ago this surprising, paradoxical, humble king rode into Jerusalem on the back of a donkey, to give himself on the cross, to die for you and me. He was gentle. He came to establish peace, to "cut off the chariot... and the war horse" and break the "battle bow" (9:9-10). But, just as Zechariah predicted, this peaceful man was attacked, struck, and pierced (13:7b; 12:10b).

This morning, our king comes again. He is present in our sanctuary, in the cross on the altar, in the symbols in our stained-glass windows, in the anthems and hymns composed in his honor, in the presence of his gathered people, the Body of Christ. Jesus is here right now, offering himself, seeking our allegiance now.

Will we give it to him? Will we make him the king of hearts? You see, the only thing any of us can either give to God or withhold from God is our love. God already owns everything else! So, to God, our worship and praise, love and loyalty — freely given — are the most valuable things in the universe!

God's situation is aptly depicted in that famous painting by Holman Hunt: Jesus Christ as *The Light of the World*. The painting is based on a verse from Revelation, "Behold, I stand at the door and knock; if anyone hears my voice and opens the door, I will come in..." (2:20 RSV).

In the painting, Jesus holds a lamp as he stands outside the fast-closed door of a believer's heart, quietly, gently, humbly, patiently waiting to be invited in. There's no latch on his side of the door. The door to our hearts can never be forced open. You and I are the only ones who can open up and let Christ in.

Jesus Christ didn't come as the king of clubs. He never tried to beat anyone into submission. He didn't come as the king of diamonds. He didn't try to dazzle with wealth or power. Jesus doesn't want to be king of anything, except the king of our hearts! His self-giving is evident. His love is powerful. It can change our lives.

Jesus rode into Jerusalem on Palm Sunday and died on a cross on Good Friday to win your love and mine. Will we give it to him? Will we open the door and invite him in? Dictators come and go. Empires rise and fall. Great nations expand in influence and then eventually and inevitably recede. Yet for 2,000 years the man on the donkey rides to us to give himself in love, ask for our loyalty, and invite us to follow him.

This morning can we say with the author of our first hymn,

> *Redeemer, come! I open wide my heart to you, here Lord abide! Let me your inner presence feel; your love and grace in me reveal. So come, my (king); enter in! Let new and nobler life begin your Holy Spirit guide (me) on, until the glorious crown (is) won.*
> ("Lift Up Your Heads, O Mighty Gates," Georg Weissel, 1642)

Behold! Your king is coming, humble and gentle! He comes to be the king of our hearts. Let him in!

---

1. http://www.preachingtoday.com.
2. http://www.sermoncentral.com.

Questions for Discussion

1. List the paradoxes inherent in the Christian message. Find verses to support each.

2. Obtain a copy of Holman Hunt's *The Light of the World*, either as a print or online. What does the artist infer about Jesus? About the inhabitants of the house? Analyze the elements of the painting: the lamp, the door, the visitor, the inhabitor.

3. Research the tradition of hospitality in the world at this time.

4. How does the book of Zechariah make its prophecy to the early Christian writers? How well does he prophesy Christ?

5. Do you believe in prophecy? Are there still prophets?

— Overview —
JOEL

Noted Old Testament scholar Bernard W. Anderson assigned a late date to the book of Joel: sometime between 500 and 350 BCE. Like Obadiah, Malachi, Haggai, and Zechariah before him, Joel prophesied in Judea during the post-Exilic period. The impetus for his ministry was a locust plague that ripped through his nation. Joel described the devastation in vivid detail. The insects' teeth were like lion's fangs (1:6b). They charged like war-horses (1:2b) and scaled city walls like attacking soldiers (2:7). The poetic nature of this book is evident in Hebrew.

But it also is discernible in our English translations. For example, verse 1:4 clearly uses repetition for affect:

> What the cutting locust left,
> the swarming locust has eaten.
> What the swarming locust left,
> the hopping locust has eaten,
> and what the hopping locust left,
> the destroying locust has eaten.

Repetition is a common poetic device found throughout the Hebrew Scriptures.

The book of Joel unfolds in three sections. Verses 1:1—2:11 describe a locust attack. Verses

2:12-17 are a sincere call to repentance. Verses 2:18—3:21 depict the coming day of the Lord. There will be terrifying portents for the latter: "The sun shall be turned to darkness, and the moon to blood" (2:31). Still Joel views the Day of the Lord as overwhelmingly hopeful. As verse 3:18 puts it, "In that day the mountains shall drip sweet wine, the hills shall flow with milk," and God will restore the fortunes of God's people.

The church has found much significance in this prophet. For example, Peter quotes from Joel at length on the Day of Pentecost (see Acts 2:17-20). Verse 2:13 frequently is used in Christian worship as an Assurance of Pardon. Curiously, Joel 3:10 reverses the better-known Isaiah 2:4 and Micah 4:3.

If the Minor Prophets are preached on once a month, as has been the pattern for this series, Joel would arrive in December. One of the great themes of Advent is Christ's second coming, which many hymns address. These include Bach's beloved harmonization of "Wake, Awake, for Night Is Flying" and United Church of Christ Pastor James Martin's contemporary hymn, "Return, My People," which was written with Joel 2:12-23 and Isaiah 11:1-12 in mind. If Joel 2:28a-29 is chosen as a focus, hymns celebrating the Holy Spirit may also be appropriate. These include a 1983 hymn text by Presbyterian Pastor John A. Dalles, "Come, O Spirit, with Your Sound" and other Pentecost hymns.

Children are concrete thinkers, and they understand rules. Just as important for them — and adults — is to experience grace. God's rules, like the Ten Commandments, and grace, go hand-in-hand. A *Peanuts* cartoon illustrates the many rules children face.

Lucy is quizzing her companions on the meaning of life. She comes to Charlie Brown, who is standing on the mound. "What is the meaning of life?" she asks. Charlie responds, "Be kind, don't smoke, be prompt, smile a lot, eat sensibly, avoid cavities, and mark your ballot carefully; avoid too much sun, send overseas packages early, and keep the ball low." Lucy stares at Charlie Brown for a moment in annoyance. Then she responds, "Hold still, Charlie Brown, for I am about to bop you right in the nose!"

Like much of *Peanuts*, these panels make a point. All of us are surrounded by a long list of expectations and rules. While most rules are for our good, no one can keep them all perfectly. There comes a time when we fail and must rely on forgiveness, grace, and the opportunity for a fresh start. That, with God's grace, these things are possible is good news for children and adults.

Good News, Bad News, Who's to Say?
Joel 2:1-3, 10-14a

There's a story that comes to us from the Taoists of China. It seems a poor farmer owned a single horse. The old man depended on this animal for everything: plowing, pulling the wagon, carrying wood, tools, and water. But one day a bee stung the horse, and it got so frightened it ran away to the mountains. The old farmer searched for his horse but couldn't find it. His neighbors came and said, "We're sorry to hear your bad news, losing your horse."

"Bad news, good news, who's to say?" was the farmer's response.

A week later his horse came back, accompanied by twelve wild horses that had followed the farmer's horse back from the mountains. Twelve more horses: this was a real windfall for the farmer! Excitement spread through the village. The neighbors came over to congratulate the farmer on his good news.

"Good news, bad news, who's to say?" was his response.

The farmer had one son. The son decided to break the wild horses so they could be sold at market. But while he was trying to break one of the horses, he was bucked off and broke his leg. The neighbors came by: "Bad news, your son getting hurt."

The farmer's response was — you guessed it! — "Bad news, good news, who's to say?"

Two weeks later a war broke out between two warlords. A squad of soldiers from the warlord in the farmer's district swept through the town. They conscripted every able-bodied man under fifty to fight on their side in a battle. But because the son was laid up with a broken leg, he didn't have to go.

That probably saved his life. Every other young man in the village who was drafted at that time was killed. One of the points of this story is good news and bad news can be two sides of the same coin. It depends on how you look at things.

You see that same two-sided coin with most of the Minor Prophets. Their messages are mixtures of good news and bad. Take the day of the Lord: We find warnings of an impending, terrible disaster, a coming Judgment Day from A to Z — Amos to Zephaniah — in the Minor Prophets.

Remember Amos? He warned God would dismantle his nation. No one would escape. It would be as if a man ran away from a lion at night and instead bumped in to a hungry bear. Or made it to his house safely, only to put his hand on a poisonous snake (5:19).

Remember Zephaniah, the "scandal in sandals" who preached like he was "baptized in vinegar"? He predicted a coming "day of wrath, a day of distress and anguish, a day of ruin and devastation, a day of darkness and gloom" (1:15).

So also Joel, writing maybe 300 years after Zephaniah, offers bad news. Consider the scripture:

> *Blow the trumpet in Zion; sound the alarm... Let all the inhabitants of the land tremble, for the day of the Lord is coming, it is near — a day of darkness and gloom, a day of clouds and thick darkness... nothing escapes.*
> (Joel 2:1-2a, 3b)

(sounds like Zephaniah, right?) Bad news! Really bad news!

But then there's a glimmer of hope. Joel continues:

> *(E)ven now, says the Lord, return to me with all your heart, with fasting, with weeping, and with mourning; rend your hearts and not your clothing. Return to the Lord, your God, for he is gracious and merciful, slow to anger, and abounding in steadfast love.*
> (2:12-13)

Some of you will recognize those two last lines as a commonly used Assurance of Pardon. Joel concludes, "Who knows whether (God) will not turn and relent?" (2:14a).

There you have it: a summation of the Not-So-Minor Prophets! They present a double-sided coin of bad news and good. In warning of judgment ahead, they're realistic. Because the troubling truth is, you and I are judged. We all eventually must answer to God: a holy and righteous God who can't ignore our sins.

Karl Menninger, in his bestseller *Whatever Became of Sin?*, writes about a "stern-faced, plainly dressed man (who) could be seen standing still on a street corner in the busy Chicago Loop. As pedestrians hurried by on their way to lunch or business (the man) would solemnly lift his right arm, and pointing to the person nearest him, intone loudly the single word 'Guilty!' Then he'd drop his hand and point to the next person, and shout, 'Guilty!' One man said, 'But how did he know?' "[1]

The hard reality is all of us are guilty! Take the Ten Commandments. We all agree that these guidelines for godly living are great! We agree we need them. But do we keep them? Always? No.

Is there anyone here who claims she or he keeps every one of the commandments all of the time? That they've always honored their father and mother, never ever taken the Lord's name in vain, always remembered the Sabbath and kept it holy, never skipping worship once, never coveted, never ever, ever told a lie? If so, please raise your hand. No hands.

We don't even give the Ten Commandments lip service! When we take God's name in vain, or tell a lie, or bear false witness by spreading gossip, we break one of the commandments with our lips. Jesus takes the Ten Commandments even further! In the Sermon on the Mount he tells us not only not to kill, but not even to get angry, not only not to commit adultery but not even to look with lust, not only not to swear falsely but not to swear oaths at all (Matthew 5:21-24, 27-28, 33-37). That's keeping the Ten Commandments times ten!

We're all guilty of breaking God's commandments. That's no joke! God created the universe to run on certain physical laws, like the law of gravity. If you jump off the Empire State Building, you don't break the law of gravity. It breaks you.

Likewise God gave us these guidelines for godly living. When we break them, we break them at our peril. In the process, we break our relationship with God and each other, we destroy community, and we break ourselves. The crime is serious. The punishment is death. The bad news is God, the law giver, can't overlook sin.

But for Christians, good news is proclaimed most clearly not in the prophets but in the gospels. The word gospel in Greek means "good news," as you know. The amazing good news is that in Jesus Christ, God acted decisively to overcome sin and conquer its consequence, death. God has done for you and me what we can't do for ourselves. In and through Christ, God has acted to save us. In fact, in Hebrew, the name Jesus means "God saves."

The price of our salvation is high. It cost Christ the cross. We call the day he died Good Friday. But it was a bad day for him. The cross was a brutal instrument of torture. It wasn't designed only to kill, but to crush the victim's spirit, and cow everyone who saw it.

Cold spikes nailed hands and feet to the wood. The crucified was stretched out and defenseless, exposed to biting insects and the burning sun. You didn't die from blood loss but from slow suffocation, which could take three days. Many went insane with pain before they died.

Bad news for Jesus was good news for us. What did Jesus say as he died? His first word from the cross was "Father, forgive them, for they know not what they do" (Luke 23:34 RSV). Father, forgive them, for they know not what they do! That's astonishing!

Having experienced in his own body the worst that men and women can do, having been the innocent victim of the greatest injustice in history, Jesus looked at sinners — like you and me — and forgave! Jesus our judge also is our Savior! That's good news!

Jesus offers forgiveness. He can see the beloved, precious child of God hidden beneath the grime of guilt and slime of sin. He knows the worst about us, but loves us still. Good Friday clearly speaks of God's long-suffering forgiveness and love.

Fredrick Buechner writes about this. He notes:

> *(T)he one who judges us most finally will be the one who loves us most fully. Romantic love is blind to everything except what is lovable and lovely, but Christ's love sees us with terrible clarity and sees us whole... The worst sentence love can pass is that we behold the suffering which love has endured for our sake and that is also our acquittal. The justice and mercy of the judge are ultimately one.*[2]

How should we respond to this love? Three centuries ago a young German nobleman pondered the cross of Christ. Count Nicholas von Zinzendorf knelt alone before the altar in a country chapel. As the rays of the sun cast shafts of light through the lovely stained-glass windows he poured out his heart to God.

Before him was a crucifix, a cross with Christ

on it. Underneath it were inscribed these words: "All this I did for you. What have you done for me?" The young nobleman pondered those words. Then and there Count Zinzendorf committed his life to Christ.

He gave up a vast fortune and a comfortable diplomatic position for a life of Christian service. In the course of his life he wrote several well-loved devotional classics, which still are read today. He composed more than 2,000 hymns. He also supported and protected the Moravian Church, which was a persecuted minority.

Preaching salvation through the cross of Christ became the cause — and joy — of Zinzendorf's life. He wrote:

> Our method of proclaiming salvation is this: to point out to every heart the loving lamb, who died for us, and although He was the Son of God, offered himself for our sins... by the preaching of his blood, and of his love unto death, even the death of the cross, never... to digress... from the loving lamb: to name no virtue except in him, and from him and on his account, to preach no commandment except faith in him... no other happiness but to be near him... no other self-denial but to be deprived of him... no other calamity but to displease him; no other life but in him.[3]

For Zinzendorf, Jesus was all-in-all. Jesus was good news that allowed him to become good news for others.

Good news, bad news, who's to say? Life is a mixture of good and bad, isn't it? But for Christians, the bad is far outweighed by the good. The powers of sin and death are strong and depressing. But God's love, forgiveness, and salvation are stronger still. As Paul puts it in Romans, "(W)here sin increased, grace abounded all the more" (5:20). In the end, nothing will be able to separate us from the love of God in Christ Jesus (8:39). The bad news is: judgment is real. The good news is: for those who cling to the cross of Christ, judgment is swallowed up in love. Thanks be to God!

---

1. Karl Menninger, *Whatever Became of Sin?* (New York: Bantam Books, 1978), pp. 1-2.
2. http://www.episcopalcafe.com.
3. http://moravians.org.

Questions for Discussion

1. How is a Christian to accept good news? Bad news?

2. Do you believe that the human condition is inherently flawed?

3. Examine the Ten Commandments. Are they still useful? Valid? Which do we choose to address? (Or shall we give up?)

4. What of a society that flaunts these laws? What can we expect?

5. What is the "good news"? What of "judgment"? As the forces of two sides continue to play out, how can we get on the right side?

Annotated Bibliography

Achtemeier, Elizabeth. *Preaching from the Minor Prophets* (Grand Rapids, Michigan: William B. Eerdmans Publishing Company, 1998). By a respected Presbyterian (U.S.A) scholar and longtime Adjunct Professor at Union Theological Seminary in Virginia. Provides historic and theological context for each of the Minor Prophets. Lists recommended commentaries. Offers up to a half-dozen sermon suggestions for each prophet.

Anderson, Bernard W. *Understanding the Old Testament.* 4th Edition (New York, New York: Prentice Hall, 1986). A classic, written by a United Methodist scholar who taught at Colgate Rochester Divinity School, Princeton Theological Seminary, and Boston University School of Theology, and at major universities. A favorite for undergraduate surveys of the Hebrew Scriptures but also useful at graduate level. Unmatched for its concise presentation of a complex subject. A revised, 5th edition available since 2006.

Boice, James Montgomery. *The Minor Prophets,* Volumes 1 and 2 (Ada, Michigan: Baker Books, 2006). Accessible yet scholarly and in-depth treatment of each of the Minor Prophets. Connects the prophet's message to challenges facing the Christian and churches today. By the longtime Senior Pastor of Tenth Presbyterian Church in Philadelphia, who was the principal speaker on The Bible Study Hour for more than three decades.

Buttrick, George Arthur, ed. *The Interpreter's Bible*, Volume 6 (New York, New York: Abingdon Press, 1956). A standard reference for preachers and teachers. This twelve-volume series offers a general introduction to each of the Minor Prophets, plus exegesis and exposition for individual passages. Updated New Interpreter's Bible published in 1996.

Heschel, Abraham J. *The Prophets: An Introduction* (New York, New York: Harper and Row, 1969). Justifiably famous study of the phenomenon of Hebrew prophesy by a scholar from the Jewish Theological Seminary in New York. Covers topics such as the prophet's self-understanding and sense of calling. Reviews the Major Prophets in depth. But also devotes chapters to Amos, Hosea, Micah, and Habakkuk. Reissued in 2001.

Kelly, Balmer H., ed. *The Layman's Bible Commentary*, Volumes 14 and 15 (Atlanta, Georgia: John Knox Press, 1977). Passage by passage survey of each of the Minor Prophets. In terms accessible to the average reader. But sufficiently scholarly to provide a background for preaching and teaching.

Scott, R.B.Y. *The Relevance of the Prophets* (New York, New York: The Macmillan Company, 1973). General introduction to Hebrew prophesy. Includes chapters on the antecedents and beginnings of prophesy in Israel, plus prophetic theology. Closes by addressing how these figures speak to our time. By a United Church of Christ, Canada, pastor and Princeton University professor also noted for his hymns.

Small, Jill H. *Back in the Days of Prophets and Kings: Old Testament Homilies for Children* (Denver, Colorado: The Morehouse Group, 1997). A United Church of Christ pastor offers children's lessons on Old Testament figures, including all the Major Prophets and seven Minor Prophets. This book is well thought out, engaging, and energetic.

Journals

As noted in the Preface, the Minor Prophets are not often chosen as first readings in the Revised Common Lectionary. Still, they do appear. Helpful lectionary-based journals include:

Emphasis, CSS Publishing Company, Inc., 5450 N. Dixie Highway, Lima, Ohio 45807, www.csspub.com or www.sermonsuite.com. Available online monthly. Provides multiple illustrations for all three readings.

Lectionary Homiletics, Lectionary Homiletics — Preaching Conference, Inc., PO Box 1866, Midlothian, Virginia 23113, www.goodpreacher.com, covers theological and pastoral themes related to one chosen lesson each week, plus sermon reviews, art connections, scripture and screen and a sample sermon. Published bi-monthly.

Online Subscription Service

StoryShare, a division of www.sermonsuite.com, offers stories for every lectionary reading.

www.ingramcontent.com/pod-product-compliance
Lightning Source LLC
Chambersburg PA
CBHW071721090426
42738CB00009B/1838